D1602610

6/18/99

Culture, Biology,
and Sexuality

Culture, Biology, and Sexuality

Edited by David N. Suggs and Andrew W. Miracle

Southern Anthropological Society Proceedings, No. 32

Michael V. Angrosino, Series Editor

The University of Georgia Press

Athens and London

Southern Anthropological Society

Founded 1966

Published by the University of Georgia Press
Athens, Georgia 30602
© 1999 by the Southern Anthropological Society
All rights reserved
The paper in this book meets the guidelines for
permanence and durability of the Committee on
Production Guidelines for Book Longevity of the
Council on Library Resources.

Printed in the United States of America
03 02 01 00 99 C 5 4 3 2 1
03 02 01 00 99 P 5 4 3 2 1

Library of Congress Cataloging in Publication Data

Culture, biology, and sexuality / edited by David N.
  Suggs and Andrew W. Miracle.
    p.   cm.—(Southern Anthropological Society
  proceedings ; no. 32)
    Includes bibliographical references.
    ISBN 0-8203-2058-7 (alk. paper). —
  ISBN 0-8203-2059-5 (pbk. : alk. paper)
    1. Sex customs. 2. Sex (Biology) I. Suggs,
  David N., 1956– . II. Miracle, Andrew W.
  III. Series.
  GN484.3.C84   1999
    306.7—dc21   98-27029

British Library Cataloging in Publication Data available

Contents

Preface   vii
David N. Suggs and Andrew W. Miracle

Human Sexuality: The Whole Is More than the Sum of
Its Parts   1
Suzanne G. Frayser

Sexing Anthropology: Rethinking Sexual Culture,
Subjectivity, and the Method of Anthropological
Participant Observation   17
Gilbert Herdt

Theory and the Anthropology of Sexuality: Toward a
Holistic Anthropology in Practice   33
David N. Suggs and Andrew W. Miracle

Talking Love or Talking Sex: Culture's Dilemma   49
William Jankowiak

Faster, Farther, Higher: Biology and the Discourses
on Human Sexuality   64
Carol M. Worthman

Human Sexual Behavior and Evolution   76
Linda D. Wolfe

A Discussion of Culture, Biology, and Sexuality:
Toward Synthesis   86
Ernestine Friedl

APPENDIX: Sex the Invisible   90
Ernestine Friedl

List of Contributors   109

Preface

David N. Suggs and Andrew W. Miracle

There is every indication that the anthropology of sexuality is finally undergoing professionalization and that it is growing in relevance in the discipline. Every year we see an increasing number of articles and books devoted specifically to sexual studies. There are more doctoral students working in the area (although still far fewer than one might hope), and in the last few years there have been several conferences devoted to sexuality and culture. These developments are the result of a complex interaction of historical factors: the feminist movement, the gay and lesbian rights movement, and the advent of AIDS, to name only a few. In the anthropological study of sexuality, there is already an array of theoretical orientations and methodological approaches that is much more bewildering in variation than this volume demonstrates.

This symposium was originally designed to provide a forum from which we might look to research examining the biological and cultural interface in sexuality and to explore why anthropology has not been able to achieve more integration of biological and cultural or of behavioral and ideological approaches to understanding human sexuality. We admit to having given participants a great deal of leeway in how they might contribute toward those aims, but we did in some measure achieve both of those goals. Our presentation of rough drafts of these papers at Kenyon College in October 1996, and the attendant discussions on the following day, were productive in creating themes of integration in what otherwise might seem a diverse collection of articles.

The first theme is summarized by Ernestine Friedl's "Sex the Invisible." For obvious reasons, there is a lack of observational data in the study of human sexuality. Friedl provides such an insightful backdrop for the papers in the symposium that we have reproduced her article in this volume to encourage those who have not read it to do so. The papers by Herdt and Suggs and Miracle address that issue most directly, but Frayser and Jankowiak also deal with ideation and behavior in ways influenced by Friedl's argument. The second theme is that of the relationship between biological and cultural influence. Both Wolfe and Worthman clearly address that issue; however, the implications of method and theory for making such connections are also discussed by Frayser, Herdt, and Suggs and Miracle. In addition to that collective value, the individual papers present a wealth of theoretical, methodological, and substantive material.

Herdt's work focuses on the question of whether a detached subjectivity in fieldwork is problematic for an anthropological understanding of sexuality. Beginning with the notion that we have not had many opportunities to observe the intimacies of sexual behavior, he discusses the methodological problem of relying strictly on people's reports of their behavior. He then discusses the notion of sexual identities, pointing out how research on sexual identity can obscure our understanding of erotic encounters, especially given the tendency to assume that similar ideologies will yield similar behaviors, and a strongly ethnocentric current in ethnographic treatments of sexuality to date. Herdt then suggests that attempts to correct our privileging of ideology over practice in the realm of sexuality are difficult to evaluate. "Sexing anthropology," as he refers to the process, "has introduced a host of problems that entangle not only our epistemology of cultural worlds, but the means by which we stake a perspective as fieldworker on these worlds." Looking at those problems in discussions of "power and sexuality" and "sexual cultures," he concludes that—problematic or not—careful methodological innovation is necessary for the further development of the field.

Noting that the concept of holism has been a distinctive feature of anthropology, Frayser calls for a more integrated treatment of sexuality. She suggests that overspecialization into subdisciplinary niches is responsible for a lack of discussion across the interests of social, cultural, biological, and psychological approaches. She also reviews the cultural context out of which anthropological studies of sexuality have emerged. She argues that "the emergence of sex as a cultural concept was tied to the definition of a naturalistic world, the research and development of the scientific community, the shift to a consumer economy, and interpretations of the self in society at large." She then reviews the epistemological, theoretical, and methodological variation within anthropological studies, noting the significant challenges to holism found in the tension between the goals of scientific or humanistic anthropology and their often conflicting efforts toward generalized explanation and particular interpretations. Her conclusion emphasizes the continuing usefulness not only of ethnography but also of cross-cultural work, and she offers some suggestions for developing a more holistic anthropology of sexuality.

Suggs and Miracle look at some of the metatheoretical problems in the development of the anthropology of sexuality, arguing that basically incommensurate paradigmatic assumptions have prohibited discussion across theoretical boundaries even when the will to do so has been explicitly pronounced. They suggest that we continue to construct theories in ways that demand a replay of the "nature/nurture" controversy, even though most of us agree that both biology and culture interact to produce our behaviors. The remainder of the paper presents a critique of the authors' own theoretical orientation (cultural materialism). They suggest that an inadequate conceptualization of individual agency and the role of ideation in cultural continuity prohibit effective discussion with biological anthropologists on the one hand and with interpretive cultural anthropologists on the other. The authors conclude with some tentative suggestions for theoretical revision and a call for a greater metatheoretical awareness and refinement in anthropology at large.

Noting that no culture achieves a very comfortable synthesis or reconciliation between "romantic love" and "erotic sex," Jankowiak claims that every culture is nonetheless compelled to attempt one. His paper explores the range of cultural responses to sex and love, as well as the regulation of their interrelationship. On the basis of cross-cultural review, Jankowiak suggests that there is a gender bias in preferred metaphors for talking about sex and love, one which he argues is relevant for understanding our own society's construction of sexual propriety. While "official American culture" stresses the de-eroticization of love, "popular or underground American culture" celebrates the eroticization of love. He therefore concludes that because "this debate wears a class face, the legal situation has not resulted in a cultural consensus concerning the appropriate language in which to converse about the sexual encounter."

Wolfe's work begins by considering the long-term evolutionary events that yielded sexual reproduction and ultimately the sexual biology of primates and humans. She reviews the origins of internal fertilization and hormonal regulation in reproduction. She then discusses the changes in sexuality that emerged with the catarrhine and allocatarrhine primate lines, noting both similarities to and differences from humans. She reviews the origins of female orgasm and same-sex sexual encounters, arguing that both are clearly present among primates. She demonstrates that with regard to sexual behavior humans are "fairly average catarrhines." Moreover, "the differences between ourselves and the other primates are not so much in the underlying biology . . . [or] mating behaviors but in the cultural meanings humans attach to their sexuality."

Worthman's paper, more than any other in this volume, represents a true blend of the biological and the cultural in both data and analysis. Beginning with a discussion of a *Newsweek* magazine article on life course and sexual potency, Worthman considers both the "public" digestion of new hormonal research and the actual implications of that research from a bioanthropological perspective. She asks how our culture shapes our construction of biology, even as the academy recognizes biological influence on behavior. As with her previous work, Worthman's insightful perspective promises greater awareness of the interactive effects of biology and culture on sexuality.

Friedl has generously summarized for us her discussion comments at the symposium. Her understanding of the significance of this collection, as well as her thoughtful comments on individual papers, are presented here as a conclusion to this volume.

When the Southern Anthropological Society asked if we were interested in organizing the key symposium for the 1997 meetings, we saw it as an opportunity to address a need that we had been discussing for some time. During 1992, while editing *Culture and Human Sexuality*, we began talking about the need for a conference of anthropologists studying sexuality. We made plans to approach granting agencies after Suggs returned from the field in 1993. That year, Suggs met Gilbert Herdt for the first time at the American Anthropological Association meetings in Washington and sought his advice on the organization of a conference and about potential grantors. As always, Herdt was kind and generous, and gave us some good ideas.

While we were searching for funding, the invitation came from Tim Wallace, then president of the SAS, and we saw it as a further opportunity to achieve our aims. We proposed the key symposium that resulted in this volume. We continued to seek support for a gathering of the symposium contributors before the SAS meetings.

If our peers do not always take anthropological studies of sexuality seriously, President Rob Oden and Kenyon College do. Oden generously agreed to support a two-day meeting in October 1996, footing the bill for travel, lodging, and food for all the symposium participants, as well as space for closed-door meetings. In return, we agreed to read the papers to the campus first and opened that day to the community at large by invitation and advertisement. Each participant in the symposium and each contributor to this volume has individually expressed his or her gratitude not only for the financial support, but also for the graciousness with which Kenyon College fed us and housed us. All of us benefited not only from the presentations of draft papers but from our discussions on the following day. We believe it was one of the most productive days of academic exchange in which we have ever been involved, a sentiment echoed by several of the participants. As a member of the faculty of Kenyon College for a decade now, Suggs takes this opportunity for a personal word of thanks to Oden and the college's faculty and students, who helped make the final versions of these papers so very much better by their support of our initial gathering.

We are also very grateful to the people who helped us manage the conference and the symposium. Sharon Duchesne and Zoe Foster were instrumental in the organization of the meetings, the production of the programs, and the necessary mailings. Tom Collins (University of Memphis) graciously and successfully managed the local arrangements for the SAS. We appreciate his sage advice and tireless efforts on behalf of the SAS. Daryl White deserves a similar word of thanks for his outstanding work as the SAS secretary and for his help and advice in the organization of our meeting. We are especially indebted to Michael Angrosino for his patience and support as SAS Proceedings editor.

Finally, the members of the Southern Anthropological Society deserve words of thanks and praise. For some time now, the SAS has proven itself to be the most vibrant of the regional organizations for anthropologists. The attendance at the meetings was heartening, and the discussion of the individual papers and of the symposium itself was enlightening and enjoyable. We are grateful to those in attendance for their support for our ideas, and we appreciate their willingness to engage as a group in an anthropological consideration of sexuality.

Culture, Biology,
and Sexuality

Human Sexuality: The Whole Is More than the Sum of Its Parts

Suzanne G. Frayser

How paradoxical it is that anthropology, traditionally defined as the holistic study of human beings, has had to rediscover sexuality. In "Anthropology Rediscovers Sexuality: A Theoretical Comment," Vance (1991:875) notes that anthropology's relationship to the study of sexuality is "complex and contradictory." Indeed, "the discipline often appears to share the prevailing cultural view that sexuality is not an entirely legitimate area of study, and that such study necessarily casts doubt not only on the research but on the motives and character of the researcher. In this, we have been no worse but also no better than other social science disciplines."

The relative paucity of systematic information about sexuality in ethnographies attests to anthropologists' apparent reluctance to investigate the topic, despite their self-imposed designation as "fearless investigators of sexual customs and mores throughout the world, breaking through the erotophobic intellectual taboos common in other, more timid disciplines" (Vance 1991:875). As an heir to this characterization, I was surprised when I found little anthropological theory and few concepts or data specific to sexuality as I embarked on cross-cultural research on this topic. "Ambivalence and even avoidance of the topic continue, and it is still difficult to 'separate the kernel from the chaff' and 'maintain any perspective' while sifting through the massive amount of information and opinion related to human sexuality" (Frayser and Whitby 1987:xix–xx). Okami (1990) describes how difficult it can be to define the line between scholarly literature and advocates' materials, so central have sexual issues become in the political arena.

A review of the literature on sexuality over the last century reveals how disciplinary specialization defines and narrows the aspect of sexuality studied (Frayser and Whitby 1987:xix–xxx; 1995). Developmental theories in psychology focus more on cognitive and moral development than on normal childhood sexual development (Frayser 1994). Sociological theories about sexuality minimize the influence of biology (e.g., Reiss 1986; Laumann et al. 1994). And biological theories concentrate on sexual behavior as one aspect of reproduction, reproductive strategies, or genetic makeup (e.g., Margulis and Sagan 1986, 1991).

In light of this state of affairs, I agree with Vance (1991:875) that anthropology has "been no worse but also no better than other social science disciplines" in studying sexuality; however, anthropology can and should do better. More than any of the social and behavioral sciences, anthropology has staked out the holistic study of human beings as its distinctive disciplinary territory. If we define human sexuality as a system composed of biological, social, cultural, and psychological attributes that intersect in producing erotic arousal and/or orgasm, and associated with but not necessarily resulting in reproduction, then it seems to be a perfect topic for anthropological investigation. The interaction among the biological, social, cultural, and psychological attributes of human sexuality creates a dynamic that makes it possible to study sexuality as an integrated whole rather than as a set of loosely connected factors.

Based on our knowledge of human evolution as well as worldwide social, cultural, and psychological diversity, we anthropologists are in a better position than those in any other discipline to provide a meaningful perspective on sexuality as a whole. This is not to say that we can claim detailed expertise for the whole. Rather, anthropologists can contribute a *perspective* characterized by multidimensional inquiry, open to a variety of explanatory options that can incorporate biology, society, culture, and/or psychology. The core of this integrated approach includes questions about more than one dimension, data and expertise from other disciplines when necessary, and analysis of variations in cultural concepts that define aspects of sexuality within and across social groups. Concentration into niches of specialized expertise may be blinding us to the interconnections so critical and distinctive for the definition of the discipline in general and the study of sexuality in particular. Or it may be that we no longer share paradigmatic assumptions that underlie the traditional ideal of holism and are in the process of defining a new type of discipline.

Anthropology has not rediscovered sexuality as a whole, but only portions of it. It has yet to discover sexuality as a rich, multidimensional field to which the traditional holistic perspective of anthropology can be applied. This conclusion raises questions about why anthropologists have not been leaders in the study of human sexuality and what role they can or are willing to play in this field. The response to these queries requires an examination of the cultural context in which the study of sex and anthropology as a discipline emerged.

INFLUENCES AT THE TURN OF THE NINETEENTH CENTURY

At the end of the nineteenth century, anthropologists faced the challenges not only of defining their new discipline but also of adapting to a shift in worldview. Like other Westerners, they tried to make sense of the social and cultural diversity that increased worldwide travel showed them, the social and cultural changes that industrialization brought with it, and Darwin's *On the Origin of Species* (1859) and *The Descent of Man* (1871), which implied that humans were subject to the same principles of nature that applied to other animals.

They confronted the demise of geographical and intellectual isolation with an uneasy recognition that the spiritual guidelines of the past were giving way to a search for patterns of meaning in nature itself. Doctors became the new priests in a world increasingly defined in physical terms according to the canons of scientific research. Central to their quest for new understanding in a changed world was the challenge of reconciling materialism, biology, and science with an equivocal Judeo-Christian sexual heritage. Under the influence of the Platonic dualist philosophy of the Greco-Roman empire, Christians separated the spirit and the flesh, giving priority to the spiritual over the physical (Lawrence 1989).

Sexology developed in tandem with the social and behavioral sciences and a more pronounced naturalistic view of the world. Cultural and social changes channeled both the conceptualization of sex and research about it. Sex gained importance as a separate and relevant domain of human expression, marked by its codification as a distinct cultural category. In *The History of Sexuality* (1978), Foucault describes a widening interest in sex during the Victorian era, despite its reputation for sexual repression. Professional and ordinary discourse included sex, if only by omission or inclusion in definitions of abnormality, which added to its power as a distinctive realm of activity. In *Consuming Desire* (1988), Birken describes how cultural changes dovetailed with economic shifts to explain why sexology developed when it did. He locates the beginning of sexual science with the emergence of a consumer culture between 1871 and 1914. He claims that Darwin's redefinition of biology qualified him as "the real founder of sexology" because he "discovered desire as the fundamental ground of both sexes" and portrayed a state of nature where there "were only genderless, desiring creatures" (Birken 1988:7). Birken links naturalistic explanations stemming from biology with economic change. He suggests that Darwin's theory of biological evolution reinforced the new consumer economy because it was "the elemental basis for a new conception of individualism based on desire itself" (Birken 1988:7). Birken expressed the social shift from a production to a consumer-based economy by noting that individuals were changing their economic decisions from wanting what they needed to needing what they wanted, the latter limited only by the extent of their desires.

Early sexologists supported the idea of natural patterns by attempting to discover the natural laws of sex (e.g., Krafft-Ebing 1978; Freud 1962). They used science to legitimize the study of sex and adopted a biomedical emphasis in the process, a continuing trend expressed, according to Irvine (1990:28), in the work of Kinsey and his associates (1948, 1953) and of Masters and Johnson (1966, 1970).

The cultural context of the late nineteenth and early twentieth centuries shaped the development of scientific interpretations and theories, including those about sexuality. Anthropologists shared in the fashionable paradigms of the day. Social evolutionists (e.g., Morgan 1964) used models from biological evolution to explain social and cultural diversity, but distanced themselves from the people they studied by labeling them "savages" or "primitives." Sexual customs (for example, polygyny and nudity) often served as convincing markers of the uncivilized status of the natives.

In *On Becoming Human*, Tanner points out how Victorian cultural beliefs about men and women affected the assumptions of scientific theories about sex. Tanner (1981:1–10) shows how Darwin's theory of sexual selection became a scientific justification for a new origin myth that supported the prevalent Victorian view of passive women who played no part in the development of human society. Likewise, in *Sexual Science* Russett (1989) documents the ways in which researchers used science to confirm women's inferiority, thus maintaining a cultural status quo despite movement for social change in women's roles. As Fausto-Sterling (1985) demonstrates in *Myths of Gender*, scientists continue to incorporate cultural biases about gender in their scientific research and theories.

The widespread cultural belief that normal sexuality entails reproduction also became an important assumption in many theories about sexuality at the turn of the century. Middle-class norms sanctioned marriage as a package of interconnected prescriptions for love leading to marriage, which entailed having sex for producing children and establishing a family, headed by the father and nurtured by the mother (Cancian 1987). Non-reproductive activities such as masturbation stood out as dangerous behaviors that could result in mental illness or physical maladies. Women who showed too much interest in sex by masturbating qualified themselves for surgical removal of the clitoris (Degler 1978:388). In *The Female Malady*, Showalter (1985:55), a historian, describes how the reproductive process itself could impair a woman's mental well-being if it was not properly balanced. Although men, as moral inferiors to the asexually superior women, were allowed more latitude in sexual expression, their health might be impaired if they did not conserve their sperm for reproduction (Baker-Benfield 1978).

Just as the social organization and cultural concepts of Western society affected the ways in which scientists interpreted sexuality, scientific theories influenced the culture at large. In *Idols of Perversity*, Dijkstra (1986) shows how artistic representations of women in the early years of the twentieth century used evolutionary theory to justify misogyny and reinforce the social order. By showing women as narcissistic, as childlike, or as identified with the natural order, these representations diminished women's social roles; by highlighting women's sexual energy, artists portrayed women as uncivilized threats to men's intellectual superiority. In *Never Satisfied* (1986), Schwartz, a historian, describes the symbolic implications of medical regulation and scientific measurement for individuals in terms of their body image. For example, Detecto scales allowed individuals to compare their weight with acceptable scientific standards, a metaphor for the increasing domination of scientific conclusions as a route to "the truth" about individuals.

In sum, the emergence of sex as a cultural concept was tied to the definition of a naturalistic world, the research and development of the scientific community, the shift to a consumer economy, and interpretations of the self in the society at large. Individuals began to include sex as one criterion by which they defined themselves, and physicians incorporated it as a basis for assessing abnormality, thus legitimizing its relevance to individuals.

These close connections of sex with psychological definitions and cultural boundaries at all levels of society may account for the power and danger that sex has assumed in the last hundred years. As Douglas (1966) defined it in *Purity and Danger*, symbolic dirt is anything that is out of place. Professionals and laypeople alike in the culture of the United States are still searching for the appropriate place for sexuality. Perhaps that is why so much sexuality is regarded as dirty. When sex crosses implicit boundaries of the culture, it becomes dirty—abusive, dangerous, wrong. As Campbell (1986) demonstrates in her overview of the sexual advice literature for young adults from 1892 to 1979, sex education materials reiterate themes of sexual danger, whether from masturbation, prostitution, and venereal disease at the turn of the century, or from STDs, sexual violence, and unplanned pregnancies today. In addition to scholarly treatises on the state of contemporary sexuality, the prevalence of pornography, bodice-ripper romance novels, sexually titillating advertising, violence-laced musical lyrics, sexual victimology, and homophobia testifies to the ambivalence and disease-laden imagery with which Americans regard sexuality.

INFLUENCES FROM SCIENCE AND OTHER DISCIPLINES

More specific reasons that anthropology may not be in the forefront of sexuality research stem from its ambivalence about its role in science and its identity as a discipline. Debates about particularism and generalization in both method and modes of analysis illustrate this struggle. Anthropological theory at first expanded the biological model of evolution to explain social and cultural variation. But these evolutionary paradigms gave way to social and cultural functionalism as fieldwork became a defining feature of social and cultural anthropology. A particularistic emphasis on the distinctive configuration of the social and cultural characteristics of a group led to interpretations of sex as one part of the social order, usually subsumed by wider social institutions such as marriage, the family, and religion. This approach to the study of other societies, a quasi-objective method, inhibited anthropology's contribution to the study of sexuality and confused its role in the scientific enterprise.

Herdt and Stoller (1990:17) argue in *Intimate Communications* that participant observation, "the umbrella approach for anthropologic fieldwork," circumvents subjectivity by requiring the fieldworker to be a participant but to hold back from fully participating in a group so that he or she can objectively observe it. The inherent distance between the researcher and the people studied precludes in-depth considerations of sexual experiences, the individual meanings of which are subjectively structured. This traditional approach to fieldwork and ethnography may partially explain the dearth of data on sex in ethnographies and the limited information on sexuality in terms of institutions and kinship categories.

Moreover, the concentration on particularistic studies of individual groups has hampered sexuality research by inhibiting the formulation of generalizations. Unless we assume that one group represents the social organization or culture of all groups, we cannot generalize from it. Some anthropologists have difficulty accepting the need for systematic cross-cultural research based on a sample of societies chosen to represent cultural diversity at different times and in different geographical locations. Because context has become so integral to research in cultural and social anthropology, removal of information from its context seems an affront to fieldworkers' meticulous descriptions and theoretical formulations at the local level. However, *not* using these careful descriptions in cross-cultural research is an affront to the discipline as a whole, because it stifles our ability to generalize, gain credibility for our findings, and perceive the gaps in our research methods and theoretical concepts.

Shifting from particularism to generalization can create emotional angst over the apparent epistemological conflict between them (Frayser 1996). Nevertheless, both field research and cross-cultural research are viable anthropological methods that can contribute to developing knowledge within a scientific framework. One does not detract from the other; each can enhance the other.

For example, when I began the research for *Varieties of Sexual Experience* (Frayser 1985), I decided to look at sexuality as a system in and of itself, related to but not subsumed by the usual institutional frameworks of marriage, the family, or the economy. I hypothesized that if sexuality were a system, then there would be clusters of interconnections between different variables that might fall outside the usual conceptual categories. I found that the benefits of the process of cross-cultural research center on category assessment, contextual evaluation of descriptions, recognition of bias, articulation of specific bases for generalization and theory-building, and identification of transcultural patterns within local contexts (Frayser 1985:423–51).

Category construction for cross-cultural research involves deconstruction of familiar concepts like marriage or the family, so that the attributes are precise and can be identified in a variety of social settings. They cannot be so culturally specific that they would exclude most variations. This approach does not detract from the definition of marriage within a specific group; rather, it allows the researcher to assess the degree to which a local group's definition of marriage shares attributes with other groups. The analysis demonstrates the most common patterns and does not assume their configuration in advance.

Cross-cultural research reveals biases throughout the extant research literature. I found wide gaps in the literature on what I regard as basic topics, for example, menstruation, intercourse, and homosexuality. Information about sexual behavior is often located under such conventional categories as marriage, family, kinship, and religion. Thinking about the pattern of gaps and the location of information prompted me to consider how much investigators' interpretations of sexuality were biased in terms of reproduction, with little discussion of nonreproductive sexual behavior.

Cross-cultural research and detailed fieldwork reinforce each other. Cross-cultural research is only as good as the information on which it is based. The more detailed and complete ethnographers are in their descriptions, the more sophisticated the hypotheses that can be tested by cross-cultural researchers, who can thus identify gaps in the anthropological literature that fieldworkers can subsequently fill.

The anthropological concentration on particularistic descriptions and analyses of social and cultural aspects of groups also leads to the omission and/or neglect of physical, biological dimensions of behavior. Like cross-cultural research, biology and biological anthropology offer another type of broad framework for interpreting human behavior in general and sexual behavior in particular, because they draw our attention to the shared aspects of being human.

Analysis of sexual and reproductive anatomy and physiology complements social, cultural, and psychological information to make sense of the questions about and data regarding human sexuality. What is *human* about human sexuality? How does biology affect psychology and vice versa? Is our sexual functioning purely a product of our construction of our behavior? What is normal and how do we decide?

Medical texts and works in biological anthropology provide direction and raise questions about how physiological processes are affected by social interaction, cultural definitions of normality, and individual cognitions, perceptions, and emotions. Nevertheless, they contain numerous gaps. For example, there has been little discussion of the link between sexual response and breastfeeding. Instead, medical articles concentrate on the nutritive properties of breast milk, bonding between mother and infant, and the physiological mechanics of breastfeeding. The erotic breast disappears into a reproductive context. Medical discussions highlight the disadvantages of a primarily physical, scientific perspective without the added dimensions of psychology, culture, and society. Yet they are a rich resource when we seek to track definitions of sexual normality, abnormality, and their indicators.

Sex by Prescription (Szasz 1980), a work by a psychiatrist, points out the pitfalls that physicians and educators encounter when they claim authority for defining normal or correct behaviors on the basis of their limited and often uninformed perspectives. Likewise, Irvine (1990) chronicles the dangerous biases that sexologists grounded in medical discourse bring to the study of sexuality. This may be one reason that the humanist, experiential contingent of sexologists has developed and vied for prominence in the professionalization of sexology.

Biological anthropology, particularly the study of human evolution, provides a productive resource for investigating what is *human* about human sexuality. Examination of sexual and reproductive attributes shared with other animals leads to an appreciation of humans' place in the animal world as well as to an identification of humans' distinctive features. Human biological traits, which accentuate evolutionary trends in reproduction (for example, menstruation and a longer infant dependency period), also lay the foundation for the development of culture and psychology, which then affects aspects of anatomy, physiology, and the adaptation to the environment.

When I first studied culture and psychology, I thought of them as the pinnacle of human development, much as Bronowski lauds cultural developments in *The Ascent of Man* (1973), as if biology fell off the rocket of progress and burned up in outer space. Now I think a more fitting metaphor is that of a rope, the strands of which wrap tightly together to give strength to the whole. Culture and psychology dance with society and biology to produce the complexity and dilemmas that we face in dealing with human sexuality as a whole.

Ford and Beach's *Patterns of Human Sexual Behavior* (1951) stands as a valuable example of the merits of interdisciplinary collaboration and attention to the biocultural bases for human sexuality. I strongly disagree with some of the conclusions about human sexuality derived from a sociobiological model, but I think that they raise provocative questions with which we must deal rather than discount. In *The Evolution of Human Sexuality* (1979), Symons integrates cross-species data with information from the human evolutionary record to posit ingrained psychological traits that emerged from human adaptations and affect sexual behavior today. He notes how inimical to cultural and social anthropologists his findings may be because they challenge the learning paradigm so entrenched in the social and behavioral sciences. In *Anatomy of Love* (1992), Fisher, a biological anthropologist, suggests why adultery has been adaptive for humans, despite monogamous mating patterns, and how patterns of marriage worldwide support the survival of children. On the basis of findings from comparative primatology, Hrdy concludes that sexually passive or uninterested females were the women who never evolved (1981:176, 182).

These studies challenge widely held assumptions about the sexual "nature" of men and women as well as deeply held moral beliefs and disciplinary paradigms. Underlying some of the responses to the theoretical formulations and research findings of biological anthropologists and psychologists may be the fear that their findings undermine the meticulous analyses of cultural anthropologists about the dominance of culture. On the other hand, some may fear that because some behavior may be explained in terms of biology, then all behavior has to be confined to this level of explanation. Claims that a form of sexual behavior is "natural" may serve as rationalizations for unjust social arrangements or unfounded stereotypes. Accusations of reductionism and essentialism are sometimes well placed, but they do not make the relevance of biology or materialism go away.

As Perper points out in *Sex Signals* (1985), biology is not a fixed, unalterable force but a dynamic interplay of living organisms involved in change, activity, and functional behavior. Given this dynamic, it would be surprising if biology did *not* relate to social, cultural, and psychological aspects of sexuality. The work of Money, a psychologist, demonstrates the power of an integrated model of gender (Money 1988; Money and Ehrhardt 1977).

The systematic study of human sexuality that I proposed in *Varieties of Sexual Experience* benefited from my examination of evolutionary theory and biological research, which aided me in defining the characteristics of human sexuality and then identifying some of the variables that I thought would be productive to investigate cross-culturally. Because humans engage in more nonreproductive sexual behavior than most animals, I argued that sexuality was broader than the reproductive framework that is often used to define it. If sexuality is equated with reproduction, this is more a matter of cultural definition than of biological fact. This conclusion led me to consider whether there were clusters of variables distinguishing more reproductively defined societies from more sexually defined ones. Some of the major findings from my research were based on the distinction between social and cultural patterns of reproductive and nonreproductive behavior.

More recently, I reviewed the professional literature to develop a model for defining normal childhood sexuality (Frayser 1994). Given the intense personal, political, and professional investments in the issue, I wondered how to assess the material in a balanced way. A holistic framework is particularly useful in the study of such socially charged and culturally taboo topics. It allows us to step back from our cultural assumptions and consider the gaps in our formulations. I therefore guided my inquiry using the holistic framework of anthropology, organizing information into biological, psychological, and sociocultural categories. Examination of the evolutionary foundations of sexuality helped me to weigh some of the cultural biases that I share about the topic.

I do not, however, see the biological aspect of sexuality as "the basic material—a kind of universal Play Doh—on which culture works, a naturalized category which remains closed to investigation and analysis" (Vance 1991:879). Rather, I view biological aspects of sexuality as a systematic framework of findings and theory from which I can begin to explore the interplay of shared sexual patterns, whether they be social, cultural, or biological. The questions I ask center on defining how biology and culture contribute to understanding a specific or general pattern of human sexuality. Privileging one dimension or setting up competition between dimensions becomes a red herring that distracts us from the study of human sexuality as a whole.

DEALING WITH THE WHOLE

Given the patchwork of research on human sexuality in anthropology, how do we approach human sexuality in an integrated way? A Native American psychologist, Terry Tafoya, in a plenary speech at the Society for the Scientific Study of Sex, said that we may assume that a system of knowledge may also be a system of ignorance, because emphasis on certain ideas and behaviors entails ignoring or eliminating others. Applying this insight to anthropology's study of sexuality, we have chosen to concentrate on too narrow a range of social and cultural aspects of sexuality, thus minimizing, ignoring, or isolating ourselves from the physical and biological aspects.

Tafoya also said that we can have context or definition but not both, meaning that the more we streamline a definition to apply cross-culturally, the less context remains. To deal with this dilemma, we need *both* cross-cultural research and fieldwork as mutually supportive methods to identify shared social and cultural patterns across societies and to demonstrate the distinctive ways that humans organize their societies and cultures into meaningful units for the participants.

Finally, Tafoya commented on the value of cross-cultural research, which allows us to see through someone else's eyes, but recommended that we never give up our own eyes. In other words, we need to balance our immersion in other contexts with valuing our own perspective and context. This is a difficult challenge for anthropologists who study human sexuality today. How do we maintain our vision as a discipline, upholding our definition as the holistic study of human beings, while immersed in our specialized corners of research, whether we are engaged in fieldwork in another culture, in specific analysis of a form of social construction, or in laboratory study of nonhuman primates or fossil remains?

In reflecting on what we can do as a discipline, I have come back to the question of why I decided to involve myself in a field so professionally marginal and culturally charged. My response to the question of what we can do partially derives from my own reasons for becoming a cultural anthropologist. My roots are in the South, centered in the traditionalism of the capital of the Confederacy, Richmond, Virginia. Structure, civility, a deep sense of family and history, and definite gender roles guided my early life. My colleague Anne Bolin describes the South as "the land of the repressed." Perhaps that repression accounts for my ongoing interest in religion, which has been augmented by a concentration on human sexuality, a topic avoided in polite company but embraced in steamy, neurotic scenes by southern writers and in the behavior of southerners who try to maintain a clear distinction between public and private behavior. Some inklings that I would go beyond the established structure were my fascination with the writings of adventurers/explorers like Richard Halliburton and Thor Hyerdahl, identification with Susan Hayward's role as a brave woman in the movie *White Witch Doctor*, and dreams about ancient times in Egypt. When I was twelve, I announced to my classmates that I wanted to be an anthropologist when I grew up. Even then, holism appealed to me, because I believed I could study any aspect of humanity I chose to. Anthropology held the promise of breaking out of the conventional structure in which I grew up and of moving into new and different worlds. I still hold those beliefs, and I still think that anthropology can fulfill its promise.

My anthropological research on human sexuality is about crossing boundaries and refusing to accept structures imposed on me, whether lovingly or unkindly. I also think that being able to cross boundaries invests anthropologists with a powerful approach. When I consider the powerful role that anthropologists can play in the study of human sexuality, I recall what Victor Turner, one of my mentors in graduate school, said about ritual symbols—that they have sensory and ideological poles of meaning, the former drawing on bodily experiences and sensations, the latter structured according to cognitive processes. The power of symbols derives from the juxtaposition of these and other levels of meaning, for they are multivocal, not competitive. Anthropologists can study these juxtapositions of meaning.

I also think of Turner's own attempts to reconcile structure with lack of structure, both theoretically and personally. In *The Ritual Process* (1969) he discusses the alternation between the social organization necessary to structure our lives so that we can effectively participate in society, and times of marginality when we experience a lack of structure in a temporary but meaningful space in time. It is during such marginal times, free from the ordinary bonds of structure, that we can share in the fullness of our humanity, in *communitas*. As anthropologists, we need to engage in *communitas* when we study human sexuality. By crossing the usual boundaries that separate us within the discipline and from other disciplines, we can truly discover human sexuality.

REFERENCES

Baker-Benfield, C. J. 1978. The Spermatic Economy: A Nineteenth Century View of Sexuality. In *The American Family in Social-Historical Perspective*, 2d ed., ed. M. Gordon, pp. 374–402. New York: St. Martin's Press.

Birken, L. 1988. *Consuming Desire*. Ithaca, N.Y.: Cornell University Press.

Bronowski, J. 1973. *The Ascent of Man*. Boston: Little, Brown.

Campbell, P. 1986. *Sex Guides*. New York: Garland.

Cancian, F. M. 1987. *Love in America*. Cambridge: Cambridge University Press.

Darwin, C. 1859. *On the Origin of Species by Means of Natural Selection*. London: Watts.

———. 1871. *The Descent of Man and Selection in Relation to Sex*. New York: D. Appleton.

Degler, C. N. 1978. What Ought to Be and What Was: Women's Sexuality in the Nineteenth Century. In *The American Family in Social-Historical Perspective*, 2d ed., ed. M. Gordon, pp. 403–25. New York: St. Martin's Press.

Dijkstra, B. 1986. *Idols of Perversity*. New York: Oxford University Press.

Douglas, M. 1966. *Purity and Danger*. London: Routledge and Kegan Paul.

Fausto-Sterling, A. 1985. *Myths of Gender*. New York: Basic Books.

Fisher, H. 1992. *Anatomy of Love*. New York: Norton.

Ford, C. S., and F. Beach. 1951. *Patterns of Sexual Behavior*. New York: Harper and Brothers.

Foucault, M. 1978. *The History of Sexuality*, vol. 1. New York: Random House.

Frayser, S. 1985. *Varieties of Sexual Experience*. New Haven, Conn.: HRAF.

———. 1994. Defining Normal Childhood Sexuality: An Anthropological Approach. *Annual Review of Sex Research* 5:173–217.

———. 1996. The Essential Tension Between Particularism and Generalization. *Cross-Cultural Research* 30(4):291–300.

Frayser, S., and T. J. Whitby. 1987. *Studies in Human Sexuality*. Littleton, Colo.: Libraries Unlimited.

———. 1995. *Studies in Human Sexuality*, 2d ed. Littleton, Colo.: Libraries Unlimited.

Freud, S. 1962. *Three Essays on the Theory of Sexuality*. New York: Basic Books.

Herdt, G., and R. J. Stoller. 1990. *Intimate Communications*. New York: Columbia University Press.

Hrdy, S. B. 1981. *The Woman That Never Evolved*. Cambridge: Harvard University Press.

Irvine, J. M. 1990. *Disorders of Desire*. Philadelphia: Temple University Press.

Kinsey, A. C., W. B. Pomeroy, and C. E. Martin. 1948. *Sexual Behavior in the Human Male*. Philadelphia: Saunders.

Kinsey, A. C., W. B. Pomeroy, C. E. Martin, and P. H. Gebhard. 1953. *Sexual Behavior in the Human Female*. Philadelphia: Saunders.

Krafft-Ebing, R. von. 1978. *Psychopathia Sexualis*. New York: Stein and Day.

Laumann, E. O., J. H. Gagnon, R. T. Michael, and S. Michaels. 1994. *The Social Organization of Sexuality*. Chicago: University of Chicago Press.

Lawrence, R. J. 1989. *The Poisoning of Eros*. New York: Augustine Moor Press.

Margulis, L., and D. Sagan. 1986. *Origins of Sex*. New Haven: Yale University Press.

———. 1991. *Mystery Dance*. New York: Summit Books.

Masters, W., and V. Johnson. 1966. *Human Sexual Response*. Boston: Little, Brown.

———. 1970. *Human Sexual Inadequacy*. Boston: Little, Brown.

Money, J. 1988. *Gay, Straight, and In-Between*. New York: Oxford University Press.

Money, J., and A. A. Ehrhardt. 1977. *Man and Woman, Boy and Girl*. Baltimore: Johns Hopkins University Press.

Morgan, L. H. 1964. *Ancient Society*. Cambridge: Harvard University Press, Belknap Press.

Okami, P. 1990. Sociopolitical Biases in the Contemporary Scientific Literature on Adult Human Sexual Behavior with Children and Adolescents. In *Pedophilia*, ed. J. R. Feierman, pp. 91–121. New York: Springer-Verlag.

Perper, T. 1985. *Sex Signals*. Philadelphia: ISHI Press.

Reiss, I. L. 1986. *Journey into Sexuality: An Exploratory Voyage*. Englewood Cliffs, N.J.: Prentice-Hall.

Russett, C. E. 1989. *Sexual Science*. Cambridge: Harvard University Press.

Schwartz, H. 1986. *Never Satisfied*. New York: Free Press.

Showalter, E. 1985. *The Female Malady*. New York: Pantheon Books.

Symons, D. 1979. *The Evolution of Human Sexuality*. New York: Oxford University Press.

Szasz, T. 1980. *Sex by Prescription*. Garden City, N.Y.: Doubleday, Anchor Press.

Tanner, N. M. 1981. *On Becoming Human*. Cambridge: Cambridge University Press.

Turner, V. W. 1969. *The Ritual Process*. Chicago: Aldine.

Vance, C. S. 1991. Anthropology Rediscovers Sexuality: A Theoretical Comment. *Social Science and Medicine* 33(8):875–84.

Sexing Anthropology: Rethinking Sexual Culture, Subjectivity, and the Method of Anthropological Participant Observation

Gilbert Herdt

A revolution in the anthropological study of sexuality has been building for a generation. Its manifesto is that to better understand people's sexuality, the fieldworker must get involved in and close to their sexual lives, possibly including sexual encounters with the natives. The idea is revolutionary in several ways—scientific, political, psychological, ethical—and for many scholars it is unsettling as well. If Malinowski can be claimed as the father of the anthropology of sexuality, and Margaret Mead as its mother, I think it would be true to their own scientific worldviews to say that our ancestral parents would scold us for this idea, inasmuch as it means tampering with the policy "Don't touch the natives." You might object and say, well, sure, that's what they wrote in their books, but perhaps they had sex on the sly with some of their friends in the field. Malinowski's diaries, published in 1967 in expurgated form, at least hint of powerful sexual fantasies regarding native women. Mead (1972) is totally silent on the issue in her autobiography. But we can be sure of their fundamental opposition to sexual interaction with the natives, for it goes against all the dictates of cultural relativism in anthropology. Nevertheless, although anthropology as a discipline is supposed to be objective, and although fieldworkers are expected to exhibit a kind of detached subjectivity, it is nonetheless rumored that anthropologists have long engaged in surreptitious sexual relations with local people. If fieldworkers did indeed engage in such behavior, they could not have come right out and said so. We might as well label this the "Don't ask, don't tell" model of sexual anthropology.

Sexual study in anthropology and the other social sciences poses some special challenges to theory and methodology that we are only beginning to face. I have detailed these factors in a recent volume (Herdt 1997), but I want to underscore some broader issues here.

The first issue is that sexual intercourse is rarely observed, nor is it easy for anthropologists to obtain eye-witness accounts. Although it is true that other areas of human life may also be difficult to observe (e.g., religious experiences, secret political or economic transactions), intimate sexual matters pose a greater difficulty. As Mead observed in 1961 in a famous article on the cultural determinants of sexual behavior, virtually all societies regard intimate sexual relations as personal or private and may shroud them in secrecy. As Ernestine Friedl (1994:833) has recently observed in her very significant article entitled "Sex the Invisible," "Ordinary, run-of-the-mill, everyday sex relations in virtually all human societies are hidden, conducted away from the gaze of all but the participants." Two generations ago, Alfred Kinsey worried over this issue in the American context. How are we to trust what people report about their own sexual behavior, he asked? In a long and critical discussion in his book on sexuality and the human male (Kinsey, Pomeroy, and Martin 1948), he suggested that distortions are always entered into what people report and recall of their past behavior. Yet Kinsey believed that what people say of their sexual behavior is more reliable than what they report regarding their sexual fantasies, and for this reason he discarded all information on sexual fantasy in the final analysis of his study of American sexual behavior, even though he was able to collect rich and voluminous material. Many social scientists still accept this bifurcation and believe that remembered behavior is more reliable than remembered fantasy, although we should regard this belief with increasing skepticism, as I shall show. What is at issue is not simply sexuality, but intimacy: what people do and say behind closed doors or in the forest where eyes cannot follow them.

A second and equally serious problem is posed for anthropology by the difference between ideology and practice. For generations, anthropologists have been attuned to the difference between what people say and what they do, to the tendency to idealize ourselves, to flatter and romanticize the cultures we inhabit in our minds and in the time and space world. It is very difficult to accept the next step, however: that in the arena of sexual behavior, there may be a strong tendency on the part of many actors to substitute the cultural ideal for what they actually do in their private and intimate sexual encounters. Doing so involves us in power relationships and the social regulation of sexuality. In the context of the AIDS epidemic and the internationalization of sex research, what we know in an increasingly elaborate and in-depth manner is that people's reports of their behavior are often not isomorphic with their actual behavior. A man may report that he engages only in coital sex, but upon interrogation it is found that occasionally he also engages in anal sex with his partner. In Brazil, for example, a large household survey of five thousand respondents showed that the majority of heterosexual couples engaged on occasion in anal sex, although this fact is rarely reported in face-to-face interviews, as it is a transgression both of Brazilian sexual norms and the reproductive ideology of the Catholic church (Parker 1987).

Another aspect of this problem that is particularly important for the study of sexual cultures and sexual identities is the fact that identities are not predictive of behavior and may indeed mask or hide actual erotic encounters. For example, it is now widely known that males in many countries engage on occasion in sexual relations with other men, in spite of the fact that they identify themselves as "heterosexual" or "married" or place themselves in a social and symbolic category, such as "priest" or "shaman," that implies abstinence or the circumvention of sexual behavior. Long ago, investigators in the AIDS epidemic learned the fallacy of asking people their identities instead of asking them about their actual sexual behaviors. The reasons are obvious. If a sexual behavior is illegal, illicit, or immoral in a particular society, the most powerful sanctions are brought to bear against violators. People go to great lengths to avoid these sanctions and find ways of screening their intimate sexual encounters. Ralph Bolton, a distinguished medical anthropologist and a gay man, has long argued that this difference between identity and behavior requires that anthropologists move close to people's sexual lives, rather than relying on their verbal reports. He says that men in bath houses fill out questionnaires in which they report that they do not engage in sexual practices such as anal intercourse, or that they protect themselves with condoms if they do. In fact, however, he went into the bath houses and found that many of the same men engaged in unsafe sexual practices. When they were confronted with the contradiction between their verbal report and what they were doing, they typically rationalized their conduct by claiming that they did it only sometimes, or simply forgot to use a condom, or were inebriated, or forgot the experience, or were ashamed of what they did (Bolton 1992).

But there is another and equally powerful barrier to the effective cross-cultural study of sexuality: our own ethnocentric blinders and assumptions regarding what sexuality is and is not. This is the area most familiar to anthropology and the one in which we have made the largest contribution. The repression, sexism, and homophobia of the past have, however, harmed the investigation of the intimate and romantic and sexual in other cultures. Anthropologists who are uncomfortable dealing with sexuality at all have generally ignored this aspect of human behavior in their reports. Others who are uncomfortable with homosexuality may overlook or ignore it in their field studies. I remember one of my senior professors in graduate school twenty-five years ago advising me not to study sexuality in the field. Another professor, an expert on New Guinea societies, responded to my question about homosexuality by telling me with authority that there was no homosexuality in New Guinea. He was right, in one way, since the cultural construct for same-gender behavior in New Guinea is not labeled homosexual, nor does it have the psychosocial characteristics that we impute to this category, such as its being biologically determined, a contact only between adults, or a relationship between equals that lasts throughout life. He was wrong in another way, however, since we now know that more than fifty societies in New Guinea institutionalize what I call boy-inseminating rituals, with ordinary and frequent sexual relations between older and younger males, which occur for years (Herdt 1984).

Consider the problem of cunnilingus in New Guinea: because of the fear of menstrual blood pollution, and the misogynist character of the belief and practice system of virtually all New Guinea societies, the idea of cunnilingus is virtually unheard of. The Sambia, for example, regard the idea as repulsive and hideous, and its mere mention causes men to spit involuntarily in reaction. Maurice Godelier in 1986 commented on this attitude by saying, "Like sodomy, the very thought of cunnilingus is unthinkable to the Baruya." His statement is applicable to many other cultures. And yet Donald Tuzin (1994) has consistently reported that the Ilahita Arapesh practice cunnilingus within the intimate context of male/female sexual relations. A decade ago I questioned his report and discussed it with him, but he has insisted that the practice actually occurs, is not rare, and was always traditional, rather than being introduced in the colonial period, as I had thought.

I can now add two points to the Ilahita Arapesh report. First, there is extensive sexual variation across cultures, and we must not assume that what is absent in one group is absent in another; this assumption is another manifestation of our strong tendency in anthropology to believe that ideology predicts behavior, or to privilege ideology over practice. Second, although we may indeed find Tuzin's report credible, the fact is that he—like all other anthropologists faced with the same kind of situation—has never observed this practice. He accepts the local statement that what is reported actually occurs, when, in fact, this assertion must be taken on faith. When cultures do not code sexual conduct in the same way we do, when they practice sex but without categories of sexuality as we know them, such examples are particularly perplexing. There is, for example, the famous case of "Boston marriage" among nineteenth-century women who loved and slept with each other, and even on occasion had orgasms, but considered it not "sex" but rather "friendship." We are challenged by such examples to take into account our own assumptions, taboos, and blinders when we conduct research on sexuality.

Sexing anthropology, as advocated by anthropologists such as those who contributed to the recent anthology *Out in the Field* (Lewin and Leap 1996), will not be easy, and with good reason. Participant observation, as it was established in structural functional anthropology almost eighty years ago, meant that the fieldworker was to observe and not to change the culture under study. The time and space dictates of this position are also of interest. For Malinowski in the Trobriand Islands and for Mead in Samoa and New Guinea, detachment, "disciplined subjectivity," and an imperative not to exercise power over the natives were all attitudes that were built into the culture of fieldwork and the encounter with other cultures. The problem is not unique to anthropology. The sociologist John Gagnon (1997) has recently written that the original encounter of Westerners and non-Westerners, as exemplified in the Pacific voyages of Captain Cook, contained many interactions, including sexual ones, that were part of the colonial heritage of the expansion of the West.

THE SOURCES OF THE PRESENT

The internationalization of sexual study as a result of the AIDS epidemic is the main force responsible for this sexual research revolution, which has produced the significant problem of differentiating behaviors from identities, roles from deviances, authority—or, if you prefer, hegemonies of power that regulate sexual conduct—from the counterformation or resistance to these authorities at the site of sexuality. Among the more interesting developments of this work has been an emerging body of theory on desire, a problematization of the relationship between sexuality and gender, and the discovery in many times and places that cultural ideals do not predict actual sexual behaviors. The difficulty of understanding sexual behaviors without categories, of sex without sexuality, is particularly striking in instances of third genders that provide for religious rather than erotic satisfaction. Homosexuality and same-gender relations are among the most interesting and important of such examples, because of the spread of HIV/AIDS and the political economy of social, kinship, and religious or power relations that enter into discourse on sex.

Whatever challenges of theory these fundamentals have posed, the issues of ethnographic methodology are perhaps greater, albeit generally less discussed. Following the dictum of Malinowski (1922) that the fieldworker should observe but not change a culture, the new sexual anthropology has introduced a host of problems that entangle not only our epistemology of cultural worlds, but the means by which we stake a perspective as fieldworkers in these worlds. Critics such as Bolton (1992) have argued that such a methodology is old-fashioned and unprepared to deal with the challenges of the AIDS epidemic and the need for action anthropology in the modern world. The globalization of sex identities, commercial sex, and the commodification of the body and its iconic surfaces (through tattoos, body piercing, reproductive technologies, etc.) present unparalleled possibilities for rethinking the encounter with other cultures. Various recent books and papers suggest, then, that the anthropologist might become sexually involved with the natives, in order to grapple with the problems of privacy and cultural ideas, to establish with some accuracy the desires and experiences of local cultures and local actors. Such a position potentially violates the canon to study but not change the culture, and it also introduces a vast new set of questions about the uses of power, the role of the fieldworker in the creation of intimate relations in the field, the manipulation of this intimacy on both sides, and the ethical dilemmas and costs thereby produced.

Today, the study of sexuality might be said to encompass several main areas of intellectual inquiry, including biological elements (typically referred to as sex), learned elements (typically referred to as gender), and sexual behavior and erotics (which the dictionary defines as "that which stimulates sexual arousal"). These labels and definitions are, of course, purely conventional. In this Western formula sex is biology, gender is culture, and erotics is somewhere in between. Thus when we discuss such issues as gender identity, the development of sexual orientation and attraction, and the emergence of sexual behavior during the course of life, we begin to realize not only that these Western distinctions do not apply to the cultural classification systems of other societies (Vance 1991), but that even within our own culture, we experience significant contradictions in understanding what part of our sexual being is the product of nature and which part is the product of nurture, probably because the reality is a complex interaction of the two (Herdt and Stoller 1990).

POWER AND SEXUALITY

We might define sexual cultures as formulations of roles and norms, rules and beliefs that organize and regulate sexual conduct in the larger society. We cannot then ignore the political conditions that motivate these formations. The concept of sexual culture is therefore inherently bound by the internal contradictions of power and power relations in each context in which the sexual encounter occurs. The hegemonic husband/wife relationship of American culture, particularly as espoused by Judeo-Christian teachings in an earlier time, imagined an unequal relationship that generally eroded a sense of mutuality or companionate relations as these matters are discussed today by partners who have two incomes, two careers, and two lifeways that do not always mesh, even in bed (Herdt 1997).

It is anthropology that I will primarily address, since it is in our discipline that the most dramatic difficulties have surfaced. The anthropological study of sexuality has had a bumpy history over the past century, to a far greater extent than the public is aware. Anthropologists also have served as watchdogs over contemporary morality debates in our own society, for reasons that are not hard to find. Certainly the general taboo on discussing sex in polite company has militated against the sustained analysis of sexual behavior, since the taboo has resulted in overly clinical and medical accounts, or overly deodorized studies of sexuality. Anthropological textbooks dealt with sexuality largely in the context of reproduction, marriage, and kinship. In the functional model of Malinowski, sexuality was reduced to the needs of individual biology, whereas those anthropologists who followed the lead of Mead, Ruth Benedict, and others assumed that sexuality was covered by the act of being married, and that all other sexuality—in childhood, adolescence, in or outside of marriage, and also in later life—was either irrelevant to understanding culture, or could be handled as a problem of deviance or abnormality.

SEXUAL CULTURES

Cultural anthropology is mainly concerned with the study of what I like to call sexual cultures—their formation and meanings, their power enclaves, and the means by which social life is woven in and around sexual behavior (Herdt 1997). The concept of sexual culture is now meant to encompass that domain of beliefs, rules, and meanings surrounding sexual behavior and its regulation or conduct in a particular society and historical period. You might ask why I place such emphasis on sexual behavior, and in particular on its regulation. First, sexual relations are often of vital importance to the local definition of human nature and the cultural perception of what is normal and natural in human development (Mead 1961). Thus, sexuality is of basic concern to the local control of social personhood, and deviations from norms are approved or disapproved with consequences for many other areas of social prestige. Second, sexual behavior is potentially disruptive, indeed more potentially disruptive than other forms of resistance, in virtually all areas of human life and social organization, including economics, politics, kinship and family life, religion, and morality. We cannot escape the fundamental sense in which the social organization of sexual behavior and its social control are at the very heart of social and cultural life in virtually all human societies (Gagnon 1997).

Despite the great importance we ascribe to the sexual in the formation of culture, it is a fact that until the last decade, sexual culture was largely omitted from the ethnographies of anthropologists writing about all culture areas of the world. This omission is even more striking when you consider that in Melanesia and New Guinea, which is the area that I know the best, it is extremely difficult to conceptualize society and culture without the understanding of sexual development and sexual regulation in these cultures. The reasons typically cited for this omission include the taboo on sex in society and science (Gagnon 1989), the difficulties of eliciting accurate sexual information in the absence of observation (Herdt and Stoller 1990), the fact that sexual acts are usually private in most cultures (Mead 1961), and the ethical problems of participating directly in sexual relations with informants (Bolton 1992). For example, the inadequacies in theory, and the gaps in method and practice in the anthropological study of sexuality, surely obstructed the study of AIDS/STDs over the past decade, and hindered the construction of culturally sensitive AIDS education and prevention programs (Herdt 1992). These challenges remain; nevertheless, a new generation of scholars is emerging to tackle the relevant issues in a creative way (Brummelhuis and Herdt 1995).

In general, I think it would be fair to say that sexuality was not understood as a cultural system until the past twenty years or so, and that such an understanding occurred largely in concert with the development of gender studies, followed by the emergence of gay and lesbian studies in anthropology (Westin 1993). In fact, of course, anthropologists like me have long argued that to understand the sexual system of a culture is to offer a special window for understanding shared meanings, beliefs, and social relations in the larger society. In the new anthropology of sexuality, identified with the works of such writers as Carole Vance, Gayle Rubin, Ralph Bolton, Richard Parker, Roger Lancaster, and Anne Stoller, the ethnography is "sexed" in a way that a generation ago was characteristic of how feminist anthropology sought to "genderize" the study of culture. Take note that many of the explorers in this new field are identified as gay or lesbian, for reasons I will try to explain later. Among its hallmarks is the challenge to the theory of culture through the concept of sexual culture, which suggests that sexuality must be understood as part of cultural reality, rather than as a biological substratum of the unconscious.

Indeed, it might be argued that in the early history of anthropology,

it was the very fact of "otherness" that led to the attitude—a reaction
to colonialism, or at least its official rhetoric—that the anthropologist
should observe more than participate in the culture under study, holding
the self somewhat aloof from the nitty-gritty of such matters as sexuality. Thus, the more exotic the culture, whether in New Guinea or
Guatemala, the greater the need to remain detached. Because anthropology was seldom done in the United States or Western Europe until
recent times, no fundamental challenge to this methodological and ethical posture occurred at home. Beginning in the 1970s, however, largely
as a result of the advent of feminist anthropology and gender studies,
and then the study of people of color and cultural minorities in our own
country, this received paradigm of field study began to erode. Today, anthropologists such as Ellen Lewin and William Leap (1996) would ad-
vise that the closer we get to home—and whenever Western fieldworkers are engaged in the study of sexuality in their own countries—the
more this mantle of objectivity can be a positive barrier to understanding what is really going on in people's sexual lives.

    Anthropological studies of sexuality, beginning in the nineteenth cen-
tury, typically regarded the sexual as a product of biological evolution
(Robinson 1976). To a lesser extent, until the time of Malinowski's
functional theory of culture, the sexual was thought to be a biologically
driven individual desire that was satisfied within kinship and family organizations, the aim of which was reproduction (Vance 1991; Herdt
1984). It was, in fact, Malinowski's (1927) *The Sexual Life of Savages*
that effectively challenged the Freudian and Western model, initiating
the slow but steady process of viewing sexuality as a legitimate part of
the study of culture and society. I still regard this book as the greatest
ethnography of sexuality ever written. Malinowski demonstrated better than any previous scholar the limitations of the Western biological/
egocentric model. Trobrianders do not understand sexual excitement as
a pure product of the self isolated in the lone individual apart from social
relations and the cultural world. A variety of ethnographic works during the past generation have added to the comparative record and supported Malinowski's basic insight (reviewed in Herdt and Stoller 1990;
see also Lindenbaum 1992). Recent work on sexuality has attempted to
go beyond the notion that all erotic forms and sexual excitement are but
social constructions or enlargements of the discourse on sexuality that

would control and suppress agency and desire in culture. (See, for example, Miller 1992.) Other studies have demonstrated the limitations of a simple "cultural influence model" of sexuality that posits that sexual excitement and relations are only products of social settings (Vance 1991). Sexuality, we are beginning to "rediscover," is neither purely a product of culture nor of individual strivings and drives and power relations; the picture is more complex, especially as one takes into account the entire structure of sexuality in the course of life (Gagnon 1989). Subsequent social and cultural theory in anthropology rejected this idea and its biologism, and along with it, sexuality as an area of study was largely dropped for two generations, with the exception of Mead's (1935) New Guinea work (Vance 1991).

As formations of sociality and experience, sexual cultures create through the erotic encounters of people much of their total intentional worlds and meanings, no less than do their religion, kinship, or politics, all of which may also encompass their sexual system. The erotic experience of people as individual actors, however, resonates to social and discursive codes, and their identities may be responsive to the institutional practices and devices that constantly impinge upon them. Sexually approving and sexually restrictive cultures are typically concerned with providing not only culturally constructed sexual lifeways, but narratives for these lifeways that are part of the local theory of human nature or ontology. But because of the problematic qualities of its private character in many times and places, the sexual encounter between adults is a difficult matter to study, and, as Mead (1961) once observed, this difficulty has resulted in the conundrum that ethnographies as much as surveys of sexuality are based on hearsay, secondary reports, and words that substitute for sexual acts. And thus there may be a strong bias in the ethnological record to report cultural ideals rather than expressed behaviors in the domain of sexual culture. Where secrecy is involved—as is often the case with premarital and extramarital relationships, as well as same-gender sexuality—the problems of ideal and real are compounded. What is at stake is the positioning of erotics in the account of culture. And what we are only now confronting is the basic point that in all studies of sexuality, it is generally necessary for the fieldworker to disclose his or her identity or sexual orientation for readers to better understand the ethnography.

TABOO, AGAIN

The problem is addressed in a major way in a new book entitled *Taboo*, edited by Don Kulick and Margaret Wilson (1996). Kulick and Wilson argue that the time has come for anthropologists to respond to the challenges of the new era of disclosing sexuality by having fieldworkers tell about their own sexual encounters with the natives. Easier said than done!

Kulick and Wilson comment that they encountered a lot of resistance even to the idea of their book. They claim that white heterosexual men were the most troubled by the project; some of them not only were opposed to being in the book, but objected to its very aims and intents. They state in the preface to the book: "The only ones for whom we were repeatedly called on to justify the volume were heterosexual men, many of whom responded with suspicion or even hostility. The only people who actually tried to talk us out of doing the book (usually with the 'think-of-the-damage-this-will-do-to-your-careers' hex) were all heterosexual males" (Kulick and Wilson 1996:xii). They go on to note that "sex—their sex, the sex of 'the Other'—has always constituted one of the gaudiest exhibits in the anthropological sideshow" (1996:3). But, they counter, "throughout all the decades of concern with the sex lives of others, anthropologists have remained very tight-lipped about their own sexuality."

Esther Newton (1993:4) has suggested that the various possibilities of censorship of sexuality in anthropology are the products of academic hierarchy. According to Kulick and Wilson (1996:4): "The black hole enveloping this nonsubject serves the dual purpose of fortifying heterosexual male subjectivity by keeping it beyond the bounds of critical enquiry, and of silencing women and gays, for whom matters of sexuality and gender can never be unproblematic—who risk their stake in mainstream anthropological debate . . . and perhaps even their careers by discussing those problems too publicly." They go on to assert that "silence about the erotic subjectivity of fieldworkers also works to keep concealed the deeply racist and colonialist conditions that make possible our continuing unidirectional discourse about the sexuality of the people we study" (1996:4).

Of course, feminists, followed by gay and lesbian scholars, have had to deal with these issues in their work, and they have opened a new window on gender and sexual study by breaking with the epistemology of the past. To add the stigma of sex to the stigma of gender was too much, and it might well have aborted the movement of women into the social sciences and anthropology in particular. As Mead (1972) wryly noted about the historical conditions of women doing fieldwork in Pacific Island societies, there was a general notion that a female anthropologist should be neutered, or wear male clothes or nondescript garb, supposedly to "desexualize" her appearance, in order to blend into both public and domestic domains of women and men. Such an image—which was a part of the experience of most women fieldworkers of Mead's generation—now seems very strange. Perhaps the need to hide one's sexuality or to pass as something other than what one is will likewise seem strange to those who follow us.

CONCLUSION

The emergence of studies of sexuality in anthropology has led to a deeper sensitivity to the meaning of context and the role of the ethnographer in defining local meanings. This is a welcome corrective to the overgeneralizing tendencies of studies of sexuality in other disciplines. The Indian psychoanalyst Sudhir Kakar (1995:278) has written on the issue of desire with great wisdom. "It is assumed," he says, "that given the homogeneity of various groups in a traditional society where individual divergence within the group is minimal, the mask of desire crafted by the group's culture will also fit a majority of its members." Kakar's warning is perhaps the main lesson that I would like to draw from the disparate examples of anthropological study today. It was probably always an unwarranted assumption that the ideal culture or norm stood for the desires of the individual. Malinowski held this assumption to a degree, and Mead much more. All the models of cultural influence in this area, as Vance suggests, require attention to the meanings—personal and cultural—of sexual experience, so that we may go beyond the ahistorical and faceless normative statements of the past. Doing so entails attention to the identity and actions of the ethnographer as well; but how far should this process extend, and when is it too much or too little?

By sexing anthropology I mean the addition of sexual behavior to the ethnography, which requires us to pay some attention to the situation of the fieldworker. Intimate communications require close attention to our subjects; but we cannot sacrifice perspective in order to achieve this intimacy. The fieldworker is indeed justified in entering into the close relationships necessary to determine the difference between ideologies of sexual conduct and the realities of the person's life. But our own position is thus called into question, along with our motives. It is therefore clear that the power of the ethnographer is a definite and perhaps even causal factor in describing and explaining sexual conduct.

But this power model of culture defies the traditional "Don't ask, don't tell" model of sexual study in social science, and, indeed, it suggests a different ethic, for which we are largely unprepared. We expect students to take care in field relations, but we seldom train them to anticipate the consequences of their actions when it comes to intimate exchanges and sexual arrangements. Heightening this awareness is absolutely necessary if we are to go beyond the stereotypes of a society and its cultural assumptions about what is necessary and proper in human nature. What I find missing in anthropological accounts is an understanding and rendering of the cultural ontology of the erotic in these other times and places. Comparative studies sometimes strive for this ideal. In anthropology, we certainly have been concerned with the native's point of view. Yet one searches for the tropes that convey deeper conceptions of the person and body, psyche and culture, as these entities enlarge and constrict the local cultural reality and ideas of the erotic and homoerotic. To uncover them in ethnographic accounts, we become detectives of the perishable sensibilities that may have eluded observers and are forever in danger of being misconstrued by contemporary viewpoints.

REFERENCES

Bolton, R. 1992. Mapping Terra Incognita: Sex Research for AIDS Prevention—An Urgent Agenda for the 1990s. In *The Time of AIDS*, ed. G. Herdt and S. Lindenbaum, pp. 124–58. Newbury Park, Calif.: Sage.
Brummelhuis, H. ten, and G. Herdt, eds. 1995. *Culture and Sexual Risk*. New York: Gordon and Breach.
Friedl, E. 1994. Sex the Invisible. *American Anthropologist* 96:833–44.
Gagnon, J. H. 1989. Sexual Conduct and the Life Course. In *AIDS, Sexual Be-*

havior and IV Drug Use, ed. C. F. Turner, pp. 500–553. Washington, D.C.: National Academy Press.

———. 1997. Others Have Sex with Others: Captain Cook and the Penetration of the Pacific. In *Sexual Cultures and Migration in the Era of AIDS*, ed. G. Herdt, pp. 23–40. Oxford: Clarendon Press.

Godelier, M. 1986. *The Production of Great Men*. New York: Cambridge University Press.

Herdt, G. 1984. Ritualized Homosexuality in the Male Cults of Melanesia, 1862–1982: An Introduction. In *Ritualized Homosexuality in Melanesia*, ed. G. Herdt, pp. 1–81. Berkeley and Los Angeles: University of California Press.

———, ed. 1992. *Gay Culture in America*. Boston: Beacon Press.

———, ed. 1997. *Third Sex, Third Gender: Beyond Sexual Dimorphism in Culture and History*. New York: Zone Books.

Herdt, G., and R. J. Stoller. 1990. *Intimate Communications: Erotics and the Study of Culture*. New York: Columbia University Press.

Kakar, S. 1995. *Intimate Relations*. Chicago: University of Chicago Press.

Kinsey, A. C., W. B. Pomeroy, and C. E. Martin. 1948. *Sexual Behavior in the Human Male*. Philadelphia: Saunders.

Kulick, D., and M. Wilson, eds. 1996. *Taboo: Sex, Identity, and Erotic Subjectivity in Anthropological Fieldwork*. New York: Routledge.

Lewin, E., and W. Leap, eds. 1996. *Out in the Field*. Urbana: University of Illinois Press.

Lindenbaum, S. 1992. Knowledge and Action in the Shadow of AIDS. In *The Time of AIDS*, ed. G. Herdt and S. Lindenbaum, pp. 310–34. Newbury Park, Calif.: Sage.

Malinowski, B. 1922. *Argonauts of the Western Pacific*. New York: Dutton.

———. 1927. *The Sexual Life of Savages in Northwestern Melanesia*. New York: Harcourt, Brace and World.

———. 1967. *A Diary in the Strict Sense of the Term*. New York: Harcourt, Brace and World.

Mead, M. 1935. *Sex and Temperament in Three Primitive Societies*. New York: Dutton.

———. 1961. Cultural Determinants of Sexual Behavior. In *Sex and Internal Secretions*, ed. W. C. Young, pp. 1433–79. Baltimore: Williams and Wilkins.

———. 1972. *Blackberry Winter*. New York: Morrow.

Miller, B., ed. 1992. *Sex and Gender Hierarchies*. New York: Cambridge University Press.

Newton, E. 1993. *Cherry Grove, Fire Island*. Boston: Beacon Press.

Parker, R. 1987. Acquired Immunodeficiency Syndrome in Urban Brazil. *Medical Anthropological Quarterly* 1:155–75.

Robinson, P. 1976. *The Modernization of Sex: Havelock Ellis, Alfred Kinsey, William Masters, and Virginia Johnson*. Ithaca, N.Y.: Cornell University Press.

Tuzin, D. F. 1994. The Forgotten Passion: Sexuality and Anthropology in the Ages of Victoria and Bronislaw. *Journal of the History of Behavioral Sciences* 30:114–37.

Vance, C. S. 1991. Anthropology Rediscovers Sexuality: A Theoretical Comment. *Social Science and Medicine* 33:875–84.

Westin, K. 1993. Lesbian/Gay Studies in the House of Anthropology. *Annual Review of Anthropology* 22:339–67.

Theory and the Anthropology of Sexuality: Toward a Holistic Anthropology in Practice

David N. Suggs and Andrew W. Miracle

There has always been a tension in anthropology resulting from the diverse lifeways of our species. On the one hand, anthropologists consider their task to be the interpretation and explanation of human cultural diversity. How is it that people came to be so very different, and what makes each group's way of life distinctive? On the other hand, anthropologists consider their task to be the elucidation of what it means to be human. Underneath all the diversity is a set of biological constants and physical/environmental limitations that lead to similar, even if not identical, cultural responses. The result is some universal cultural traits and an attenuation of the degree to which we can possibly be diverse.

The tension, then, arises from the fact that well-meaning individual researchers come to focus on one or the other aspect of the discipline's task, even though we argue as a discipline that both are necessary for full understanding. Few of us have attempted to build research strategies that insist on the integrity of both enterprises. Rather, we build theories that seek either to interpret the particular or to explain the general, that attempt to examine either biological influences or sociocultural constructions. Some will go so far as to deny any validity to the one or the other. More typically, we toss off a few lines of acknowledgment to the other side of the coin.

This is truly an unfortunate state of affairs. Following on the work of the philosopher Thomas Kuhn (1962), James Lett (1987) pointed out that we are a discipline with theories that suffer from paradigmatic incommensurableness. That is, we begin with different assumptions about reality, what is knowable in that reality, and how we should know it.

If we recognized the situation responsibly, there would not be such high levels of disciplinary tension. On the contrary, we would likely hear each other and learn from each other the propositions claimed as truths by different perspectives. We might agree to disagree over which perspective yielded the most valuable approach, but we could probably live with the disagreement comfortably. We have not, however, dealt responsibly with this perspectival problem. Rather, we pretend that we are all trying to do the same thing and then we draw our battle lines at the level of strategic assumptions. We say that the postmodernists are solipsistic, the Marxists are vulgarly reductionistic, and the sociobiologists are sexist. In doing so, we make an already unfortunate state of affairs into a pitiable one by insisting on a code of jargon that identifies us as "informed" by one school of thought or the other but actually marks us as entrenched in our perspective, at least until we latch on to some other trendy approach that rises to disciplinary prominence for its brief moment in the sun.

Although anecdotes are not always instructive, we believe that the following one can serve as an example of our position. One of us recently received a damning review of a manuscript that had been submitted for publication. The reviewer began by suggesting that the paper had not "struck an appropriate balance between accessibility and seriousness." That is a symptom of our disciplinary malaise—accessibility is juxtaposed with seriousness. Do we assume that that which is readable therefore becomes meaningless? At that point, an already sorry state of affairs becomes one less worthy of sympathy than of ridicule. This is a harsh assessment, and perhaps a cynical one, but few would deny the recurrent fractious quality of anthropological debate over the past fifty years.

In this paper we question the substructure of arguments within the discipline. We imagine a research strategy that requires us to interpret the particular as well as explain the general without recourse to intentionally obtuse language. Can we allow ourselves the luxury of focusing on the particular or the general, while demanding that—at minimum—we be able to take stock of the intersection of the two?

METATHEORY AND THE ANTHROPOLOGICAL
STUDY OF SEXUALITY

Anthropologists have never found a productive intersection between structuralism and materialism, between sociobiology and postmodernism—and never will. We cannot do so for a simple reason. None of these approaches has a research design that insists that an intersection exists between the motive forces of biology and culture or between ideas and material life. Each constructs walls of epistemological assumptions that are easily scalable on one side only and that accordingly necessitate disciplinary division. We have chosen to do so as a discipline, and our struggle to communicate with one another at the most basic level reflects that choice.

Our argument looks to metatheory—the assumptions that lie beneath a theory's construction—to explore connections of the particular to the general, and the biological to the cultural. If it is radical to question the assumptions and choices of one's teachers, it is conservative to call for an anthropology that can do what it has always claimed to do: celebrate diversity through the knowledge of our singularity and to celebrate our common humanity through the knowledge of diversity—in short, to be holistic. Our argument is for the sort of disciplinary reform that will encourage us to speak to, rather than past, our differences as practitioners. It is about emboldening a discipline, one that rightly promotes tolerance of differences through the recognition of our commonality. And what better "room" in which to begin this "housecleaning" than in the developing field of culture and human sexuality?

An argument that looked at all of our disciplinary assumptions obviously would be monumental. We are most interested in discussing those metatheoretical assumptions that preclude doing both general studies of human sexuality and specific studies of the cultural construction of sexuality.

The current debates on the legitimacy of "generalized explanation" and "particular interpretation," which have emerged from the confrontation of postmodernism and scientism, have given us two broad directives as researchers. First, we have as practitioners assumed that we can be much more objective than we actually can be. At least, we have written our ethnographies in a voice that is much more objective than our methods warrant. Second, we have assumed that cultures—as whole, individual "things"—are much more systematically organized and constructed of more shared elements than may actually be the case. At least, we have written our ethnographies in ways that suggest such integrated organizations.

Does this state of affairs mean that we cannot be objective and that culture is asystematic? Is it a matter of "writing" as opposed to "doing" ethnography? The answers to those questions are important for researchers committed to promoting both the interpretive and the explanatory components of anthropological research. As the second follows logically from the first, we want to examine two pieces of work on theory and sexuality that we believe serve well to illustrate the primary problem of objectivity and systematics.

Typically bold, William Davenport (1987) has argued that there is no such thing as "human sexuality." His reasoning is clear and not without some merit. He argues that any "act sexual" is at once an "act cultural." As human beings, we cannot behave "meaninglessly," and meaning in act and belief is given to us by culture. Thus, regardless of the seeming comparability among acts of sexuality across cultures, the meaning will always be historically and particularly informed. On that basis he suggests that no two acts are strictly comparable and any attempt to compare them as human behaviors is utterly inappropriate. Although we do not dispute the historical and particular character of meaningful sexuality as experience, we believe the extremity in that position is counterproductive.

To begin, there is one confounding factor in Davenport's argument: how are we to know the uniqueness of the other in the absence of comparison? That, logically speaking, every culture is unique is without dispute. We must ask, however, *how* cultures are unique, and whether some aspects of sexual culture are unique and others not. Those questions are not, or at least should not be, matters of purely theoretical assumption. They can be, and should be, matters of empirical demonstration. It is the assumption that our task is primarily idiographic and interpretive that leads Davenport to a programmatically divisive position.

Carole Vance (1991:879) has stated, "Ecological adaptation and reproductive demands . . . explain only a small portion of sexual organization, since fertility adequate for replacement and even growth is relatively easy for most groups to achieve." This is a newer and more sophisticated phrasing of the same assumption. Regardless of the fact that fertility and other demographic concerns are at the heart of many ecological/materialist arguments, there is no need to link the concept of "ecological adaptation" directly to that of "reproductive demand and fertility." Vance's position is a simple statement of faith. Moreover, who besides sociobiologists has said that all adaptive behaviors, sexual or otherwise, must be directly "reproductive"?

Vance's landmark 1991 article, "Anthropology Rediscovers Sexuality," is an important piece of work in many ways. It points out the extent to which we have failed to professionalize sexual studies in anthropology. It also points out the extent to which we, as a community of scholars, are likely to pathologize sexuality in the face of AIDS as our biomedical (and largely physiological) models of transmission fail to consider the social construction of sex in different communities and the implications of that construction for effective control. It is also an eloquent call for a more developed anthropology of sexuality. We strongly agree with her conclusion that "we need to be explicit about our theoretical models, mindful of their history, and self-conscious about our practice" (1991:884).

Vance's vision of the future of theory in this area of study is, however, largely unsatisfactory from our perspective. To be sure, anthropology has used the terms *heterosexual* and *homosexual* as universally descriptive labels for opposite-sex and same-sex contacts respectively. Moreover, we have pretended that the terms do not possess a wealth of assumptions informed by our own embedded cultural constructions. That is, there is a subjective element in the terms that is particular to twentieth-century industrial and Western thought. In using them so casually, we have failed to emphasize the way that our own cultural baggage may not be transported to others. On that basis we can properly criticize writers of the past for assuming a substrate of behavior to be universal when it may not be. To emphasize that point is one thing. It is quite another matter to leap from there with Vance to the conclusion that opposite- and same-sex sexual behaviors around the world are incomparable except as processes of construction.

One can agree with the position that heterosexuality in Tzintzuntzan is a cultural construct that ultimately is incomparable as a whole with heterosexuality in Gambier, Ohio. Such agreement, however, does not mean that the acts upon which and out of which such constructs are built are absolutely devoid of comparative and explanatory value. Do we wish to emphasize cultural uniqueness for the purpose of particular interpretation? Do we wish to emphasize behavioral similarity for the purpose of general explanation? Most constructionists say yes to the former and tip a hat to the latter by calling forth vague notions of historical comparisons to the process of construction. Materialists and ecologists say yes to the latter and tip their hats to the former by calling forth vague notions of the former as inventive yet reflexive epiphenomena.

What would it take to say yes to both? What would it take to build an empirical examination of their interaction? It would take an approach that suggests that "ultimate" incomparability is not "utter" incomparability. The shortest route to that position is the suggestion that even though "heterosexualities" are particular constructions, the process of their construction is not itself capricious. It is more or less rule-bound with regard to adaptive potential. Such a position takes holism seriously by giving to each realm—the cultural construction and the adaptive interface with environment—motive force in the alternate realm. Such a conceptualization would require the examination of the interface between an organized system and a self-mediated experience thereof.

The question simply should not be whether heterosexuality and homosexuality are cultural constructions, for surely they are. The question is how we might conceive of same-sex and opposite-sex behaviors as comparable, for just as surely they are. As Laura Nader (1994) has recently suggested for anthropology in general, the question is not *whether* we can compare; it is *how* we might in theory as researchers construct relatively useful comparative programs for generalization in tandem with interpretive explanations of the particular cultural constructions. To suggest that we have pretended to be overly objective is apt and a fine critique. To then conclude that we can only be utterly subjective is a waste. It is nihilistic and counterproductive to an anthropology that might actually achieve holism.

As a final example, consider Vance's position on the nature-nurture debate, and how some see the "essentialist" and "constructionist" perspectives as a reemergence of that tired old controversy. In an endnote she criticizes those who "make the assertion that the debate between essentialists and social constructionists . . . is a replay of the nature-nurture controversy" as exhibiting "a profound misunderstanding of social construction theory" (1991:883). But is it? She writes, "Most observers agree that human behavior is produced by a complex interaction of biological and cultural factors; they differ on the relative weight they assign to each." This conclusion is unarguable, but she continues by saying that constructionism cannot be equated with the nurturist camp since "it encourages us to deconstruct and examine the behavior or processes which both nature and nurture camps have reified and want to 'explain'" (1991:883). Just because Vance focuses on the social construction of biological factors in sexuality, there is no reason to assume an alliance with biosocial anthropologists. Those from the hardline, hardwired behavior schools are not talking about the social uses of biology. They are talking about the motive forces of biology. It is productive to look at the ways in which cultural constructions of sexuality present the "natural state of affairs." It also is productive to recognize the extent to which our own internalized assumptions regarding the "natural" may well be the "culturally constructed." Neither of those orientations (and they are the sole means for discussing biology from the theoretical perspective that Vance presents) will allow us to explore the "complex interaction of cultural and biological factors" that, as Vance herself notes, most researchers assume to be operative in human behavior. Our point, however, is that it accomplishes little when we suggest the interaction and then build strategies for research that preclude its examination.

The irony is that most of us now cringe at the phrase "nature vs. nurture." We do so because as a discipline we have produced a wealth of data that indicate that the discussion should not be phrased in an either/or manner. Yet the fact of the matter is that the assumptions underlying our theories almost always require us in practice to treat them in an either/or manner. We therefore make innocuous references to the interaction between biology and culture—something that "we all know, of course" but that need not be examined. We treat it as a given, as an assumption that needs no empirical investigation.

To realize that there are subjective factors in any objective approach need not lead logically to the conclusion that objectivity is completely illusory. It can better be considered relatively illusory. That is, through more theoretical explicitness and self-consciousness, we can be relatively more objective than we have been in the past. We can achieve some of our goals through understanding the way that our cultural biases unintentionally have entered our discourse. But the bulk of our project can be achieved only when we responsibly build theory in ways that demand that the intersection of the general and the specific or the biological and the cultural exists and is a proper object for study.

In an atmosphere intended to promote discussion, any theoretical critique is likely to inflame passions. To minimize that possibility, we want to focus our disciplinary critique on our own theoretical inclination—the school known as cultural materialism. Since being a materialist is not particularly fashionable, it should not annoy anyone too much to indicate the ways that the construction of theory prohibits our ability to talk to other schools or subdisciplines of anthropology. We specifically suggest that materialism must be revised in at least two important ways for it to be usefully holistic: in its treatment of the relationship between the individual and society, and in its treatment of ideation and cultural continuity.

ON THE RELATIONSHIP BETWEEN
INDIVIDUAL AGENCY AND SOCIETY

To date, cultural materialism has focused exclusively on probabilistic effects on society. There has been no attempt to deal with the individual either biogenetically or as a social agent. We believe it is time to correct this flaw. We are certainly not the first to note this problem with materialism. A. F. C. Wallace (1980) pointed it out shortly after Harris published *The Struggle for a Science of Culture* (1979). More recently, Paul Magnarella, in *Human Materialism* (1993), has attempted to offer an alternative view of individual agency.

The issue is complex, to say the least. To begin, let us unambiguously state the obvious: individuals are the constituent elements of societies. It is misleading at best to talk of societies taking action. Individuals may, as a result of their various motivations, take concerted action, which may result from the participation or acquiescence of all members of a society or only a small but disproportionately influential segment.

We share Vance's opinion that "social construction work has been valuable in exploring human agency and creativity in sexuality" (1991: 877). There is much to learn from constructionist studies in this regard.

The focus of their research on discursive power and the ways that individual reformers and activists have acted against the political and symbolic interests of the more socially powerful demonstrates the interplay of individual, subcultural, and cultural forces in the construction of sexuality.

Moreover, such concerted action may give the appearance of societal unanimity. Only individuals, however, can legitimately be credited with human agency. Societies do not act. Individuals—both those who are in power and those who are not—act, alone and in concerted actions with the groups to which they ally themselves. Materialists' focus on the reified actions of "cultures," then, is a problem of particular significance to the field of sexuality.

To illustrate the morass into which that failure leads us, consider the difference between reproduction and procreation. Reproduction is the cumulative action of individuals within a society. Procreation is an act of individuals. Given the infrastructural focus of cultural materialists, it is not surprising that in their consideration of the sexual, they have been concerned almost exclusively with reproduction and the attempt by reified societies to control it. There is nothing of significance in the cultural materialist literature about the experience of sex and its meanings, or even the individual's attempts at procreation. Societal rules are, as we said above, at most self-mediated directors of action.

What is the role of nonprocreative sexuality? Here Vance's comments on the limits of "ecological explanation" centering on fertility take on some substance. Materialism has virtually nothing to say about nonreproductive acts of sexuality. While Harris (1989:237) has written of the "protean potential of human sexual needs and drives [and] the even more protean ability of human cultures to sever the connection between sexual pleasure and reproduction," there simply is no way to get at the motivations and meanings of the behaviors for the individuals involved.

From the perspective of most materialists, societies need to regulate reproduction. In cases where an increase in the labor force is adaptive, materialists have thought it a satisfactory explanation to note how societal interests in reproduction have yielded a condemnation of nonreproductive behaviors. Even if we ignore the fact that there were many different individuals and groups that built that "condemnation" (and also set aside the diverse uses to which the condemnations were put), the actions of the resulting marginalized individuals and groups have to be seen as strictly "reactions" to a reified mass society attempting to ensure effective adaptation.

One of us wanted to title this paper "Do Cultural Materialists Really Have Sex?" Is there passion and feeling in the bed of a cultural materialist? Is there neurophysiologically based pleasure? Is there even a desire to procreate? Or is there only a contemplative consideration of whether one should submit to or resist societal efforts to regulate reproduction?

If cultural materialists really have sex, then they must be aware of the experiential dimension. Moreover, if cultural materialists studied particular human sexualities more thoroughly instead of focusing generally on societies' control of reproduction, they would be aware of the extent of variation within the normatively defined behaviors associated not only with reproduction but with the erotic. They also might be aware of the tremendous range of sexual intentions and thoughts that give meaning to individual experience. Without conceptual revisions of the relationship between the individual and society, it is not possible to develop such an awareness.

ON IDEATION AND CULTURAL CONTINUITY

Sitting in a first graduate theory class at the University of Florida in 1983, one of us was interested in a particular aspect of Harris's presentation of "Culture"—interested in a critical way. The section to which we are referring reads as follows: "Rather than distinguish the mental and emic components [of the infrastructure, structure, and superstructure] according to the strength of their relationship to specific etic behavioral components, I shall lump them together and designate them in their entirety as the mental and emic superstructure" (Harris 1979: 54). Why would one do such a thing? What justifies an offhand "lumping" of the emic and mental components, given the detailed distinctions in the etic and behavioral? When asked, "Why would you do that? It seems it can only be a matter of expedience. Is it merely expedient to do it?" Harris responded directly and simply, "Yes! OK—it's expedient. So what?"

If cultural materialism has any strength, it is its ability powerfully to explain change in cultural systems. Yet fifteen years later we would say that the answer to Harris's "So what?" is that many have been disenchanted by cultural materialists' inability to explain cultural continuity in particular contexts of infrastructural change. To suggest that such continuities are relatively trivial is slavishly to believe that generalized explanation is more significant than particular interpretation. Moreover, a good deal of recent research (see, e.g., Nihill 1994) has impressed upon us the way that ideas can be sustained in changed infrastructural contexts and, more important, the seeming need for the stability available in the resulting ideational continuity.

In fairness, Harris would certainly note that materialism allows for ideological continuity as "feedback" from the superstructure in the majority of cases. He grants that in the rarest of instances ideas may be paradoxically directive of meaningful change. It is not, however, a particularly fruitful conceptualization, and it is unnecessarily restrictive of interpretive research efforts. As a corrective, one of us has recently been arguing that there is a core of ideas that never make it into the "loop" to begin with. There is no paradox in their forcefulness, no "feedback" from them; rather, there is directive, motive force—they are ideas that make change meaningful by bringing the past to the present in what Eric Hobsbawm (Hobsbawm and Ranger 1983) calls a "suitable" way.

We suggest that in any particular context it is ideational constructions centering around notions of "essential sociability" that act not as a "feedback loop" but as the primary motive force for cultural continuity within the context of change (cf., Karp 1980). While technoeconomic changes may demand a reconfiguration of the structural terrain in which "essential sociability" can be constructed, the seeming necessity and signal stability of the idea itself directs the interpretation of those changes. The historical and particular ideational core of notions of essential sociability—beliefs and behaviors requisite to definitively human interaction—allows for changes to be presented in a way consistent with the past and therefore to be made meaningful to the individuals acting in the present. In that light, Vance's well-grounded argument that we have to date simply assumed sexuality to be universally a part of essential sociability makes this line of inquiry potentially a very fruitful area of research. In short, a revised materialism could certainly make it a matter of empirical investigation that could both interpret particular constructions and offer general explanations.

For cultural materialism, the implication is that even if the bulk of significant cultural changes begin with infrastructural changes (and we believe that they do), those changes themselves are not entirely explanatory. In short, understanding the infrastructural conditions would be prerequisite to, but insufficient for, any explanation of the way that infrastructure affects structure and superstructure in particular contexts. It is not that the infrastructure directly orchestrates changes; it is, rather, that changes in the infrastructure orchestrate change probabilistically via the self-mediated direction of individuals simultaneously attempting to maintain an ideological core of essential sociability. Of course, doing so calls for a more sophisticated conceptualization of the "mental and emic components" of culture than an expedient "lumping" can achieve.

Finally, this suggestion for revision leaves us with a peculiar empathy for the experience of Julian Steward. While the ideologues of his day argued for a postponement (at best) of discussions of cultural evolution, he argued that waiting served no purpose. By analogy, even if the infrastructure is accorded a probabilistic determinative priority (and we think it should be), we do ourselves no service by not carefully dealing with ideation and its influence now. Avoiding it, we preclude our ability to talk to rather than past other schools. We ensure disagreement by choice. Steward (1972) vacillated between an infrastructural determinism and the historically particular influence of a poorly defined cultural core of ideas. We now at least understand his wavering. We do not, however, share it. The relationship between the two is best understood as one of necessary mediation between systematic adaptive demands of social existence and the compelling desire for continuity in individual experience. Even given this mediation, the ideas that we are speaking of as a "core" are capable of exact expression in the general sense. Members of all cultures have a particular ideology of "essential sociability," and behavioral observation demonstrates a limit to the range of individual interpretation. This observation leads us to the really difficult issue in sexual studies, one that our discussion at Kenyon revisited again and again.

By way of illustration, we return to a consideration of Harris's "So what?" Although his answer seemed flippant at the time, upon reflection it seems simply honest. Materialism is first a theory of behavior and always has been so. The first commitment is to empiricism. Without observation, we can build only an inferential house of culture. (Of course, honest or not, the inferential side of materialism remains problematic, perhaps particularly in the area of sexuality.) If we are able to take the postmodernist critique of culture as system to heart, how very much more inferential must it be in the absence of observation?

In fact, although we have elsewhere taken materialism to task for not focusing more thoroughly on the symbolic realms of sexuality, we are now left wondering what else it could do. That is, behavioral observation is necessary for full understanding in any cultural realm. For materialists it is behavioral observation that undermines the legitimacy of the nihilistic notion of absolutely asystematic culture. Yet as Friedl (1994) points out, we have little or no access to observational data about sexual matters. That realization actually emphasizes the importance of the focus on sexual demographics and social control, which are amenable to the observations necessary for materialism where, for example, eroticism is not.

We want to emphasize, however, that the invisibility of sexuality is not strictly a problem for materialism alone (as both Friedl and Herdt note in their contributions to this volume). The problem is not that people will lie to you. On the contrary, sensitive fieldworkers usually find willing and honest informants. The problem is that we do not behave exactly according to shared rules and beliefs, although perhaps we behave in approximation to them in most instances.

Another strength of the postmodernist critique at this level is the realization that each of us carries an imperfect understanding of what it is that we actually share in terms of rules and beliefs. Our approximations of behavior to rule are actually more accurately understood as approximations to self-mediated understandings of rules. In other areas of cultural study, we can adjust our own interpretations as anthropologists to behaviors observed against a social background. Observations contextualize and refine interpretation and inference, which is how anthropologists have traditionally understood "participant observation." In short, this realization does not attenuate the significance of observations. On the contrary, it intensifies their importance.

The importance of observations is that they help us to find the ways in which contexts shape the interpretation and manipulation of socially constructed rules. Observations direct us into those areas of inquiry that are most productive of understanding the use of the rules themselves. Without the observation of behavior and the feedback it gives us in orienting our discussions in the field, we have no way of knowing whether ultimately we are even asking the correct questions. The result is that we are bereft of the most reliable gauge of degree of system. This doubt has led some postmodernists simply to replicate running dialogues as "ethnography" on the assumption that the only system that exists is that among the researcher, the "other," and the readers. Rather than agree, we would argue that symbolic constructions and their elicitation are simply not good enough. One need not be a materialist to recognize this evaluation. As Foucault (1984:369) has put the matter: "It is not enough to say that the subject is constituted in a symbolic system. It is not just in the play of symbols that the subject is constituted. It is constituted in real practices—historically analyzable practices. There is a technology of the constitution of self which cuts across symbolic systems while using them." Yet (again, as Herdt, Friedl, and a host of others have reminded us of late), in the area of culture and sexuality research, the "play of symbols" is virtually all to which we have access.

This is not a problem for materialists alone, although it is certainly more of a challenge for them than for partisans of other schools of thought. Theirs is, after all, primarily a theory of behavior. On the other hand, the problem may be less acute when it comes to sexual studies since the dictates of materialism have led researchers to examine exactly those areas of sexuality where observational data can be brought to bear—societal reproduction rates, the demographics of sexuality, the social control of sexual expression.

Those of us who are interested in really talking to the biologically oriented anthropologists are faced with a wide methodological gulf. When the sociobiologists tell us that rules for marriage are epiphenomenal to the quest for inclusive fitness, we have data on the meaning of marriage and we have data on the actual practice of marriage. Ideals and practices together form a crucible for burning away irrelevance or establishing relevance. When they speak of "infidelity," however, we and they have only reports of such behavior. If behaviors observed without symbolic discussion strip those behaviors of meaning, symbols interpreted without observation construct meanings of purely "ideal" practice as opposed to the "actual." In fairness to Vance, perhaps that is ultimately her point. Since in sexuality we commonly have access only to symbols, it is only constructions that can be studied. If anthropology has been naive in its understanding of objectivity, however, how naive is the belief that we can understand ideation about something we cannot observe? We must work to resolve this situation—perhaps along the lines discussed by Herdt in this volume. Otherwise, we shall all have to settle for strictly inferential understandings of sexuality, a prospect that we find disconcerting.

CONCLUSION

We have tried to show that those studying human sexuality from one theoretical paradigm not only could make explicit the assumptions of that theory but could do so in a way that shows how very challenging it is to have conversations with theorists from differing schools of thought. The importance of this effort at this time is not to devise a new metatheory, nor to persuade others that one research strategy is necessarily superior to others. We remain convinced that it is essential that anthropologists begin to move once again toward holistic perspectives that will allow for cross-theoretical discussion encompassing both human similarities and human differences. Moreover, before we can begin the larger task, we must take the time to understand how the assumptions of our major theoretical schools preclude that discussion.

REFERENCES

Davenport, W. 1987. An Anthropological Approach. In *Theories of Human Sexuality*, ed. J. H. Geer and W. T. O'Donohue, pp. 100–135. New York: Plenum Press.

Foucault, M. 1984. *The Foucault Reader*, ed. P. Rabinow. New York: Pantheon.

Friedl, E. 1994. Sex the Invisible. *American Anthropologist* 96 (4):833–44.

Harris, M. 1979. *Cultural Materialism: The Struggle for a Science of Culture*. New York: Random House.

———. 1989. *Our Kind*. New York: Harper Perennial.

Hobsbawm, E., and T. Ranger. 1983. *The Invention of Tradition*. New York: Cambridge University Press.

Karp, I. 1980. Beer Drinking and Social Experience in an African Society: An Essay in Formal Sociology. In *Explorations in African Systems of Thought*, ed. I. Karp and C. S. Bird, pp. 180–96. Bloomington: Indiana University Press.

Kuhn, T. 1962. *The Structure of Scientific Revolutions*. Chicago: University of Chicago Press.

Lett, J. 1987. *The Human Enterprise: A Critical Introduction to Anthropological Theory*. Boulder, Colo.: Westview Press.

Magnarella, P. 1993. *Human Materialism*. Gainesville: University of Florida Press.

Nader, L. 1994. Comparative Consciousness. In *Assessing Cultural Anthropology*, ed. R. Borofsky, pp. 55–70. New York: McGraw-Hill.

Nihill, M. 1994. New Women and Wild Men: "Development," Changing Sexual Practice, and Gender in Highland Papua New Guinea. *Canberra Anthropology* 17(2):48–72.

Steward, J. 1972. *Theory of Culture Change: The Methodology of Multilinear Evolution*. Urbana: University of Illinois Press.

Vance, C. 1991. Anthropology Rediscovers Sexuality. *Social Science and Medicine* 33(8):875–84.

Wallace, A. F. C. 1980. Review of *Cultural Materialism*, by Marvin Harris. *American Anthropologist* 88(2):423–26.

Talking Love or Talking Sex:
Culture's Dilemma

William Jankowiak

In his autobiography the award-winning film and stage director Elia Kazan, then in his late seventies, reflected back forty-five years to a time when he shuttled back and forth between the arms of his deeply beloved wife, Molly, and the bed of the "spirited young woman" who was his mistress for many years. He acknowledged that he always wanted a secure domestic life even though he continued to be attracted to the freedom of the bachelor's existence. He knew he could not have both, because somebody would always get hurt. And yet the illusion persisted that he could have both, just because he wanted them both. He assumed that his readers would empathize with his dilemma.

CULTURE'S DILEMMA

No culture is ever completely successful or satisfied in either synthesizing or reconciling love and sex, although every culture is compelled to make the attempt. No matter how socially humane, politically enlightened, spiritually attuned, or technologically adapted the culture may be, failure is the name of the game. Some degree of dissatisfaction exists everywhere, since we rarely, if ever, realize a comfortable balance between the two. The resulting dissonance sounds in all spheres of culture. In industrial city and agricultural village alike, there is tension between sexual mores and proscriptions regarding the proper context for expressing love and sex.

Ambivalence, tension, and contradiction characterize this issue across the globe; indeed, one must be impressed by the range of responses found in different cultures. People in all societies, however, seem to share a compulsion to make a working peace with emotional love and erotic sex—to synthesize, separate, blend, discount, stress, or ignore one or the other, or both. At the individual level, the compulsion is one of personal satisfaction and emotional health, while at the social level it is one of social order and cultural survival.

Conventional wisdom holds that the sex drive, as opposed to the need for love, is the more fundamental human motive (Chagnon 1996; Small 1995). This assumption has recently been questioned by researchers exploring the interplay between sexual desire and loving intimacy (Abramson and Pickerton 1995; Gregor 1995; Fisher 1992). This research found that, in spite of the different ways cultures have sought to reconcile the two emotional orientations, one pattern stands out: sexual desire, in conjunction with its relative, romantic love, are panhuman emotions.

Because sexual gratification depends on intimate contact, the human sex urge, as Kingsley Davis (1976:223) observes, is seldom simply about achieving an orgasm. It is also about the desire for tactile contact and intimate communication with another person. It is the desire for intimacy that brings erotic interests into social relations, thereby linking eroticism with such interpersonal emotions as affection, trust, insecurity, and jealousy. In ordinary life, the two urges form a continuum that enables one proclivity to flow into the other, and vice versa. Instead of thinking of them as diametrically opposed emotions, it is more fruitful to view them as intertwining, albeit separate strains, much like the DNA helix—in effect, separate yet coterminous.

My premise is simple. Out of the stew that is our genetically based and chemically driven biological urge for sex and emotional affiliation come the psychological experiences that have been variously dubbed, defined, and distinguished as infatuation, romantic love, or simply love. When the two experiences come together, an aesthetic unity is formed. Whenever sexual desire and loving intimacy are at odds, however, a competition occurs. This competition has important implications for understanding the difficulty cultures encounter in balancing and regulating sexuality, both as private experience and as a mode of social behavior.

In this paper I will examine sexual desire and romantic passion as ideal types in order to highlight their most distinctive features. The two emotions, both individually and as an interrelated entity, present different structural and psychological dilemmas for each person as well as for the society as a whole. A range of cultural responses to the two coexisting proclivities will be explored, as will the gender bias in the preferred metaphors used to talk about love and sex. I will conclude by examining contemporary American society's oscillating position toward what constitutes a proper way of thinking about the sexual encounter.

SEXUAL DESIRE AND LOVE: ANALYTICAL IDEAL TYPES

Sexual desire, in its most objectified and abstract form, is the total pursuit of physical pleasure through the commodification of another. Not every sexual encounter is about the desire for some kind of transcendental merging with another. Some people desire nothing more than physical gratification or "release from arousal without emotional entanglements" (Abramson and Pickerton 1995:9). For individuals interested exclusively in sexual gratification, the ideal partner is anyone belonging to the individual's gender of preference who is willing, available, and nonjudgmental.

Unlike sexual gratification, love cannot be bought (or, for that matter, arranged, anticipated, or outlawed). If love is bought, it is invalidated. It is based on the perception of the unique specialness of another, and it continually seeks psychic union with that other. It is dyadic and prefers exclusivity in its emotional orientation. Gratification does not diminish a person's interest in the other. In contrast, sexual fulfillment in the absence of a love bond results in an immediate loss of interest in the other. Romantic love engenders the opposite response: sexual gratification does not lessen but intensifies interest in the other.

Because romantic love is multifaceted in its emotionality, it must be understood as a creative force possessing its own psychological configuration. It is characterized by seven mind-centered attributes or core properties that "are common to the experience of fully being in love within almost any cultural setting" (Harris 1996:86). These properties are: (1) the desire for union or merger; (2) idealization of the beloved; (3) exclusivity; (4) intrusive thinking about the love object; (5) emotional dependency; (6) a reordering of motivational hierarchies or life priorities; and (7) a powerful sense of empathy and concern for the beloved. Romantic passion therefore draws on several psychological processes ranging from erotic stimulation to emotional attachment and subjective idealization.

These psychological processes are different from those found in sexual desire. The disparity is nicely delineated in Tennessee Williams's *A Streetcar Named Desire* when Blanche Du Bois speaks to her sister Stella of her disdain for the obvious sexual appetite of Stanley Kowalski, Stella's husband. She says, "A man like that is someone to go out with once-twice-three times when the devil is in you. But live with? Have a child by?" In this case, the issues are erotic adventure and excitement versus the stability of domesticity and family. The irony in Williams's vision is that although Blanche argues for the latter as the ideal, much of her own life has been consumed by the former. Blanche's problem is not uniquely American—or feminine; Chinese literature is full of stories concerned with the difficulty in separating or blending together the two emotions. In Li Yu's *Be Careful About Love*, written before European contact, a Qing dynasty emperor is attracted to one woman's beauty, while simultaneously yearning for emotional intimacy with another. The emperor insists that "sexual love [is] a product of admiration of the other's good looks and talent [while] true love [is] the unalterable state that arises from that love" (Hannan 1988:144). The comments of both Blanche and the emperor represent the conflict at the heart of the push/pull tension between erotic attraction and a yearning for deeper emotional attachment.

At the individual level, it is the ability to personalize the love object that makes it so special yet so dangerous. This tendency accounts for one of the most perplexing of love's many paradoxes—its one-sidedness. For many there is a passage through hellish uncertainty, and, for some, there is no return. The nadir of romantic disappointment, the downward ladder, is suicide. For the Aka Pygmies, suicide may arise out of a state of extreme despondency as a result of rejection by a lover after intense wooing and special pleading. Recognizing the similar pains of romantic disappointment, the Society for the Study of Broken Hearts, established in India in 1992, proclaimed May 3 National Broken Hearts Day, a day of commiseration with and consolation for the love-afflicted.

The worst obsession of all, resulting in the most bitter pain, may come from an encounter with a seducer or seductress, a sometimes enchanting yet always dangerous Don Juan or *femme fatale*. These male and female seducers are found in stories, folklore, and cautionary tales around the world. The seducers either seem incapable of love or willfully use the love experience to manipulate and dominate their lovers. Moreover, manipulation and the incapacity to love often go hand in hand in the character of the seducer. These stories suggest that almost every culture recognizes the horrific danger of such an encounter; it can result in personal destruction as well as social chaos. Since no culture condones the overt manipulation of its members' emotional and sexual needs, the seducer, who frequently embodies the culture's concept of the ideal mate, is regarded as an immoral outlaw who is a challenge to the social order.

THE INSTITUTIONAL RESPONSE TO VALUING OR DEVALUING LOVE AND SEX

At the social level, cultures are cognizant of how human desire leads to various forms of behavior between the sexes (and between members of the same sex) that must be regulated, guided, channeled, and restricted. It does not matter whether a culture is sexually open (permissive) or closed (restrictive); the senior generation in every culture, as Alice Schlegel (1995:186) reminds us, seeks to "control the young through control over their future sexual lives." Peasant societies tend to have the strictest codes regulating premarital and marital sexual conduct, with small-scale hunting and gathering societies being the most open about pleasures found in the sexual encounter. Stratified societies have the widest variation concerning the value placed on sexual pleasure. For example, in nineteenth-century England there were multiple views on sexual enjoyment and romantic intimacy, although the aristocracy was more open and sexually liberal than the emerging middle class. The latter adopted a more reserved and sexually conservative, if not negative attitude about sensuality. Among this middle class, sexual pleasure was thought to be secondary to the formation of the love bond, whereas for the aristocracy, sex, with or without love, was pursued for its own sake (in an atmosphere of privilege and protected structure).

Whatever a culture's attitude about the value of sexual fulfillment, it must regulate sexual behavior to ensure that it does not result in force or fraud (Davis 1976). The primary means for accomplishing this end is the development of a system of norms reflecting the society's highest ideals, which always, albeit in different ways, deal with issues about family formation and biocultural continuity, according to Davis. Cultures that are not organized around dyadic bonds are based in alternative forms of solidarity, such as the lineage, the large extended family, the men's house, or, in the twentieth century, a feverish involvement in nationalistic causes. In these societies, the heterosexual love bond is held to be a potential rival to other, more important nondyadic loyalties. It is further understood that feelings of sexual attraction can lead to deeper relationships of human feeling, which in turn can develop into full-scale resistance to parental authority. In these societies romantic love is considered more dangerous than premarital sex.

To guard against the formation of unexpected love bonds, cultures have developed many forms of social regulation. Gregor (1995:338) points out that these forms can include "harem polygamy, . . . seclusion of women and chaperonage, obsession with virginity, descent systems that create primary allegiances to parents rather than spouses, clitoridectomy, the men's house complex, association of women with impurity and contamination, . . . and patterns of sexual promiscuity that undermine enduring relationships." Cultures that adopt these strategies strive to uncouple love bonds from feelings of sexual satisfaction.

It is difficult to determine how successful these strategies really are. In some instances, they are very successful, in others less so. Because sex is a private act, intimate thoughts and expressive moments, even when not culturally sanctioned, are extremely difficult to regulate. Exploratory research into the intimate domain finds it a rich communicative arena that is used for more than just the exchange of bodily fluids. Further support for this finding can be found in my cross-cultural survey (conducted with Edward Fischer) concerning the universality of romantic love. Our study found positive confirmation in 148, or 89%, of the cultures sampled (Jankowiak and Fischer 1992). This finding suggests that loving and intimacy are more common than previous scholarship had documented.

Another illustration of the difficulty in separating the two emotions can be found in the suicide rates of women living in rural areas of China

and Korea. In these societies families have successfully institutionalized arranged marriages between strangers. These families have far less
success, however, in preventing loving bonds from developing after the
marriage. Scholars have found that female suicide rates cluster into two
different age cohorts: women in their early twenties (e.g., emotionally
unattached brides) and women in their fifties (e.g., women emotionally
displaced by their daughters-in-law). This ethnographic evidence reveals how sexual and pragmatic interests can evolve into deep, loving
concern. In the final analysis, the essential difference between cultures
that officially separate sexual gratification from loving intimacy may
not be the absence of the experience as much as a restriction of the contexts deemed appropriate for its expression.

The American experiments with communal living reveal some of the
difficulties inherent in striving to prevent couples from forming bonds
of erotic love. The nineteenth-century Oneida community, for example,
idealized sexual pleasure but denied the legitimacy of romantic passion.
This viewpoint required the elders (leaders) to remain constantly vigi-
lant. Whenever a liaison occurred, the leadership transferred the individuals to different geographic locations. The Shakers represent another
instance of a group seeking to uncouple sexual desire from romantic intimacy in daily life. In this instance, the doctrine denied both emotional
experiences, only to discover that the erotic manifested in their dreams:
women, in an ecstatic state of bliss, claimed to be having sexual intercourse with God.

Scholarship focusing on the 1960s American communes that practiced group marriage unearthed similar problems and inabilities to over-
come the human tendency to form dyadic emotional bonds (Berger
1972). Another example of some of the obstacles to, if not the impossi-
bility of, transforming an exclusive feeling into an inclusive one is found
in my ongoing study of contemporary Mormon polygamy. These com
munities glorify plural or celestial marriages, while denying exclusive
or romantic intimacy between a man and even his "favorite" wife. In
over 108 families surveyed, I have not found a single example of one
that has been able to achieve this idea. Most men prefer, but do not readily acknowledge, bonding with one wife. Husbands often experience
acute guilt over their inability to uphold the community ideal of plural
but equal love and their yearnings for a dyadic bond with an individual.

The failure of this and other experiments in group marriages demonstrates the insurmountable difficulties these arrangements hold for the individuals and their society (Berger 1972:244).

LOVE, SEX, AND MARRIAGE

Love and sex, albeit separate emotional experiences, are inextricably intertwined and intimately connected. The critical question must therefore be whether they will be institutionalized inside or outside of marriage, or ignored and left to the individual to reinvent in each generation. It is not unusual for romantic love, monogamy, or individual choice to be present in non-Western societies. What is distinctive in the West is the expectation that all three factors should be combined *inside* the institution of marriage.

On these bases it is easy to infer that choice, sex, love, and marriage are nearly coterminous with one another. This is not always or inevitably so. Though it is often believed to be the case, the freedom to select a mate or a lover is not a European invention. It was long present in many tribal societies, and still is in many non-Western societies (Westermarck 1922).

Even societies that practice arranged marriages often tolerate men's and women's inclinations to choose a lover. For example, once married, men in Arab societies tended to take a second or third wife for romantic pleasure (Croutier 1989:153). As Bell (1996) points out, Taita women prefer to be the second or third wife rather than the first, because they would likely be married for love and thus would be treated better than other wives. It is apparent from these and other ethnographic accounts of polygamous cultures that "love marriages" are more frequent than previously reported. The question then becomes, What accounts for romantic passion's emergence as the primary basis, as opposed to one of many possible motives, for marriage in our culture?

Cultural materialists emphasize the structural impact of the transformation of the family from a unit of production to a unit of consumption. This process reduced kinship bonds while also providing youths with the economic and emotional resources to resist parental demands for self-sacrifice. In this situation love became the basis for intergenerational discord. It also became the impetus for defiance, whereby lovers circumvented the arrangements of the senior generation and chose their own marriage partners. Once marriage was redefined as an amorous union organized around personal choice, it entered the visible or official culture. In the Western world romantic love gradually, and in various intensities, became the language of gentility and social distinction.

THE DISCOURSES OF ROMANCE AND SEXUAL DESIRE

How a culture highlights love or sex determines which type of metaphor will be appropriate for public and private conversation. That our voice may say one thing while our body says another is one of the reasons why cultural codes regulating sexual desire and emotional interest are so hard to enforce. This is also why, during periods of intense social change, so many people are unsure of how to act in mixed company. In many instances, they become unsure of their behavior, of what signals they are sending, or if indeed those signals are being received and understood.

There are three distinct, albeit often overlapping discourses used to converse about feelings of love and sexual desire: the de-erotic, the polyerotic, and the uniromantic. Each discourse reflects a culture's synthesis of the meaning of love and sex. No matter what the culture's notion of an appropriate discourse, nonverbal expressions (particularly those that may contradict the literal ones) are subject to confusion.

Perhaps the most common discourse, the de-erotic, prefers not to use explicit sexual metaphors in public conversation, deeming them too crude and vulgar. This style is most commonly found in ranked or stratified societies, which confine sexual topics to conversations among age-mates of the same sex. On the other hand, the polyerotic style tends to accentuate sexual imagery in ordinary speech. For example, women in polyerotic cultures often respond to male sexual banter by asserting the value of their own sexuality. For them it is a source of pride and thus of their dignity. Among the Tongans, "discourse is humorous, with joking and teasing being frequently employed in conversations" (Morton 1996:176). Morton typically found that Tongan women's responses to men's sexual joking was to hit, punch, or push the men, albeit in good humor. As with any form of speech, the use of sexual imagery has numerous connotations and contexts. At times the banter can imply good-natured joking; at other times it conveys intense sexual desire or hints at secret romantic desire or attachment. On occasion the banter disguises a troubling ambivalence toward the opposite sex. With the exception of American subcultures, societies that favor the polyerotic discourse pattern tend to disapprove of public expressions of romance, affection, or love and displays of emotional intimacy. These behaviors are considered to be private matters and not open to public consumption.

In contrast, the uniromantic American pattern is organized around the notion of idealized love; it approves and glorifies public displays of affection in speech and behavior, as long as such displays are not overtly sexual. Romantic metaphors are the preferred language of courtship and public conversation, but it is understood that the love metaphors may range in meaning and implication from pure lust to unrequited worship.

GENDER DIFFERENCES IN THE AESTHETIC
OR ROMANTIC DISCOURSE

The ethnographic record shows a clear relationship between a gender's economic and political influence and the preference for a specific discourse or language pattern. This gender difference may explain why the uniromantic discourse pushed out the polyerotic in medieval Europe. When aristocratic women, the standard-bearers for eleventh- and twelfth-century European social manners, found the former more aesthetically satisfying than the latter, a new style emerged. Whatever meaning courtly love held for the individual, that style also served to establish social boundaries between the cultural elite and the peasantry. The latter enjoyed the crudities of sexual bantering, but the elite, especially its women, preferred to de-emphasize the erotic in favor of romantic imagery. In this way the earthy language of eros, or what is conceptualized as the polyerotic pattern, was replaced by the high-flown language of romance and gentility, an idiom that is used in many contexts across America today.

In our own era, Birth and Freilich's (1996) diachronic study of the transformation of Trinidadian gender relationships effectively documents the impact of disease, cultural diffusion, and social stratification on the change from the polyerotic pattern to a recognizably uniromantic pattern. In effect, they found that, at least among men, romantic metaphors had replaced sexual ones as the preferred idiom of male-female courtship and public address. The preferred idiom used to be organized around sexual imagery that regularly disguised or diminished underlying implications of romantic passion. Birth and Freilich suggest that it is Trinidadian women's newly obtained economic independence that enabled them to effect the change to romantic imagery, with its metaphors closely related to relationships, generosity, and family.

Sociological research has found that men tend to "fall in love" faster than women, who are consistently slower to make such emotional commitment (Cancian 1987). This empirical research is consistent with evolutionary theory, which holds that there are innate sex differences wherein men and women are typically attracted to different qualities of a potential lover or mate. For men the qualities are youth, health, and physical attraction, whereas for women they are ambition, social and economic success, and generosity (Symons 1979).

The attitudinal differences of men and women may account, in part, for the phenomenon of instant attraction, or "love at first sight." If erotic and romantic idealization of men is based on images of physical attraction, that also would account for men's ability to shift quickly between sexual fantasy and deep romantic affection. Women typically show more interest in assessing a man's social status or understanding his character. As opposed to physical attractiveness, these criteria have dominated females' mate selection and the formation of romantic fantasies. Since it takes much longer to evaluate character than physical beauty, women may be slower to become romantically involved or to commit completely to a mate.

Whatever the ultimate cause for the gender differences, the American legal system has upheld women's sexual aesthetics over the male's aesthetics, especially in the elaboration of the meaning and significance of sexual harassment in corporate life. American culture resonates with the same conflicts and tensions between love and sex, romance and lust, found around the world; only here the resonance is louder, more dissonant, and more complex. America is distinctive in its unparalleled and maddening diversity of competing and contradictory notions of love and sex. No other culture has ever offered such a bewildering array of attitudes and norms, behaviors and opinions, regarding sex and love. Worried signals from the entire public sector, the world of business, and the realm of academia—which together constitute the official culture—give an anxious message of propriety. Erotic reticence, sexual restraint, and individual caution are urged. By contrast, the mass-media imagery of popular culture asserts that the body and its senses are occasions for open enjoyment and frank pleasure, an attitude that mocks the official prudery of the mainstream.

In contemporary America, our dilemma over what should be the proper discourse of public conversation is compounded by the fact that all three languages—the de-erotic, the polyerotic, and the uniromantic—are used. It is common for certain American minorities to use frank erotic metaphors to speak simultaneously of romantic attraction and sexual desire, but it is deemed irresponsible, especially among members of the American professional class, to speak about the erotic in the presence of the opposite sex in the work area. The exception occurs only when there is a consenting relationship, and then only in the privacy of one's own home, among familiars, or in the semiunderground sex culture.

There have been occasional challenges to the historical link that combined sex and love inside of marriage, but it was not until the 1960s that a broadly sustainable challenge to the American ideal appeared. For the first time in American history, white, middle-class, college-educated men and women adopted the polyerotic as well as the uniromantic discourse. Twenty years later, there has been a notable negative reaction to the polyerotic language style by upper-middle-class professional women, especially when it was presented by men of their own social class. This tendency may be viewed as an attempt to censure what many considered a dehumanizing language of crudeness, and one associated with the lower classes at that. The removal of the polyerotic language from the work arena has resulted in highlighting the de-erotic and uniromantic languages, neither of which is considered ethically offensive. Furthermore, America's oscillation over the appropriateness of sexuality and its place in society is vividly manifested in the social phenomenon of "sexual harassment." The prevalence of this issue reveals society's confusion over the appropriate context for expressing sexual desire and/or conversing about sexual topics. In this context sexual harassment has become a code word for the formation of a new normative order that is concerned with when, where, and with whom the erotic may be broached in ordinary and ceremonial conversation. For American society, the ongoing shift represents a response to the excesses of "the Sixties," which sought to infuse, in the name of naturalism, the erotic into ordinary life. For many Americans sexuality remains a highly charged topic that is best left either to the privacy of the intimate domain or to the realm of comedic entertainment. In any other context, especially to the American professional class, it is considered vulgar and culturally inappropriate. From this perspective the ongoing debate over what constitutes sexual harassment can be viewed as a class struggle over the meaning of cultural appropriateness. Much of this debate has been conducted in the judicial arena, the end result being the promotion of middle-class women's sexual aesthetic as the benchmark for moral decency, good taste, and social standing.

It is easy to forget that many junior faculty who had once embraced the polyerotic speech as the language of freedom and self-assertion had, by middle age, abandoned that discourse in favor of safer modes of speech. It is ironic that when American society was most reserved in the discussion of sexual matters, many faculty members embraced the erotic as a means to demonstrate personal liberation, academic sophistication, and self-fulfillment, and for its shock value. Now that our society is more open in its discussion of sexuality than at any previous time in American history, members of the university community are rejecting the use of sexual imagery in favor of other discourse patterns. In doing so, they have made the female's sexual aesthetic indexical for elite social standing.

CONCLUSION

Although sexual desire and romantic passion are separate emotional orientations, they can easily and readily be blended together so that out of love can come sex, or out of sexual desire can develop a deep love. One can certainly exist without the other—a disheartening fact in instances when the goal is to blend the two. My examination, however, finds that without well-developed social institutions designed to ensure the separation of the two emotions, humans will be inclined to blend them. Denying the reality of this need appears to exact an enormous psychological cost.

From an institutional perspective there are many ways in which a culture can respond to the relationship between love and sex. A culture's understanding of the emotional meaning depends on its philosophy or ontology, which in turn shapes how its members come to understand the significance of love and sexuality. Whatever its cosmology, no culture can entirely prevent loving intimacy from entering into the sexual encounter, or vice versa. At best, it can only regulate the conditions for its expression.

The various trends and incredibly fast-moving shifts in American society have resulted in alternately emphasizing the romantic and the erotic, a tendency most readily manifested in the split that exists between the official American culture and the popular or underground one—the latter celebrating the eroticization of love, the former stressing its de-eroticization. Because this debate wears a class face, the legal solution has not resulted in a cultural consensus concerning the appropriate language in which to converse about the sexual encounter. The problem ensures that the underlying tensions present in our society will remain a source of contention for some time to come.

REFERENCES

Abramson, P., and S. Pickerton, eds. 1995. *Sexual Nature and Sexual Culture.* Chicago: University of Chicago Press.

Bell, J. 1996. Notions of Love and Romance Amongst the Taita of Kenya. In *Romantic Passion*, ed. W. Jankowiak, pp. 152–65. New York: Columbia University Press.

Berger, B. 1972. Child Rearing in Communes. In *The Future of the Family*, ed. L. Howe, pp. 159–69. New York: Simon and Schuster.

Birth, K., and M. Freilich. 1996. Putting Romance into Systems of Sexuality: Changing Smart Rules in a Trinidadian Village. In *Romantic Passion*, ed. W. Jankowiak, pp. 262–76. New York: Columbia University Press.

Cancian, F. 1987. *Love in America.* Cambridge: Cambridge University Press.

Chagnon, N. 1996. *The Yanomamo.* New York: Harcourt and Brace.

Croutier, A. 1989. *Harem: The World Behind the Veil.* New York: Abbeville.

Davis, K. 1976. Sexual Behavior. In *Contemporary Social Problems*, ed. R. K. Merton and R. Nisbet, pp. 146–67. New York: Harcourt and Brace.

Fisher, H. 1992. *The Anatomy of Love.* New York: Norton.

Gregor, T. 1995. Sexuality and the Experience of Love. In *Sexual Nature and Sexual Culture*, ed. P. Abramson and S. Pickerton, pp. 330–52. Chicago: University of Chicago Press.

Hannan, P. 1988. *The Invention of Li Yu.* Cambridge: Harvard University Press.

Harris, H. 1996. Rethinking Heterosexual Relationships in Polynesia: A Case Study of Mangaia, Cook Islands. In *Romantic Passion*, ed. W. Jankowiak, pp. 95–127. New York: Columbia University Press.

Jankowiak, W., and E. Fischer. 1992. Romantic Love: A Cross-Cultural Perspective. *Ethnology* 31(2):149–55.

Morton, H. 1996. *Becoming Tongan: An Ethnography of Childhood.* Honolulu: University of Hawaii Press.

Schlegel, A. 1995. The Cultural Management of Adolescent Sexuality. In *Sexual Nature and Sexual Culture*, ed. P. Abramson and S. Pickering, pp. 177–94. Chicago: University of Chicago Press.

Small, M. 1995. *What's Love Got to Do with It?* Ithaca, N.Y.: Cornell University Press.

Symons, D. 1979. *Human Sexuality*. New York: Oxford University Press.

Westermarck, E. 1922. *The History of Human Marriage*. New York: Allerton.

Faster, Farther, Higher: Biology and the Discourses on Human Sexuality

Carol M. Worthman

This paper discusses the disjuncture between current understandings of the biology of gender and sexual behavior, and the media and "pop clinical" discourses on aging. It may seem odd for an analysis of human sexuality to focus on aging, but, as is clear from popular conceptions and escalating media attention, aging serves as a lens that focuses converging cultural models concerning self, gender, and sexuality, and the relationship of biology to these factors.

GENDER, SEX, AND AGING: BIOLOGICAL AND POPULAR DISCOURSES

Over the past century the biological and behavioral bases of reproduction, including sexual behavior, have been systematically elucidated, and recent comparative biobehavioral research has de-essentialized the role of hormones in sexual and other behaviors. Those of us who study human reproductive ecology have also adopted a developmental, life history perspective that emphasizes life course trade-offs based on the importance of mortality schedules, rather than simple fitness maximization, as a key factor driving the organization of life history. Comparative research by my laboratory on lifespan endocrinology also has begun to probe the range of variation in endocrine organization of human development, reproduction, and aging.

Against this background of empirical, comparative, and deessentializing biological research, popular discourse on the role of biology in human sexuality and aging presents sharply contrasting views. This disjuncture was highlighted for me as a biological anthropologist by a feature in a recent issue of *Newsweek* (September 6, 1996) on testosterone, aging, and prophylactic hormone replacement in men. On the opening pages of the article, a lean, muscular young man on the left is eyed with envy and dismay by an apparently healthy but balding, over-weight, and worried middle-aged man on the right. Between the two men is a figure implying the "downhill" nature of the difference in their conditions. Entitled "That Sinking Feeling," a graph of percent peak av-erage output of the testicular hormone T and the adrenal androgen DHEAS by age in men shows linear decreases in these hormones be-ginning about age forty.

Falling hormone levels, the article argues, are responsible for the myriad unwelcome manifestations of aging among men. Losses of per-formance capacity—in thought, work, and sex—are emphasized, al-though the qualitative significance of these benchmarks of performance is not made explicit. Graphs in the article show that the annual number of orgasms declines precipitously with age and the angle of erection sinks to 45° to below horizontal; and we are told that ejaculatory dis-tance shrinks from two feet to five inches. Whether a higher erection angle, more frequent coitus, and greater ejaculation propulsion are, overall, either functionally significant or good or bad for well-being as the organism ages are important a priori questions that are not consid-ered, nor are the functional costs and biological trade-offs involved in these age-related changes in population averages. Rather, the American cultural metaphors linking "faster, farther, higher" to good health and social-sexual well-being in men make the biological decrements of ag-ing a parable of loss of performance, health, and thus social value.

Underlying this moral tale of the perils of decline are the physiolog-ical functions attributed to hormones. By a fallacy of association that is as old as the nineteenth-century beginnings of endocrinology, the pat-tern of age-related change in the "male" hormones, the androgens T and DHEAS, are assumed to cause rather than covary with senescence and longevity. If androgens are conceptually equated to youthful masculin-ity, then the less androgen, the less masculinity or youthfulness. The chain of association leads to the logical conclusion that hormone re-placement will prevent aging and prolong life.

In speaking about "the alchemy of love and lust," Theresa Crenshaw claims, "You don't have to go through menopause or viropause any more. . . . We can prevent them" (cited in Cowley 1996:70). William Regelson, author of a book on "the superhormone promise," states that aging is "not a normal life event but a disease," and that "it is possible to slow and even reverse the aging process" (cited in Cowley 1996:70). A veritable armamentarium of hormonal "magic bullets" is available to replace "lost" hormones and to dispel the specter of mortality. By contrast to the enormous concern over estrogen replacement, there is remarkably high demand among men for testosterone and DHEAS supplementation, despite the fact that, as the caption in *Newsweek* notes, "the treatments are largely untested" and their health value and cost are not established by any current epidemiological criteria for assessing pharmacological efficacy and risk. Nonetheless, the notion of hormones as causal agents of youthful sexuality, attractiveness, and health is so powerful that the idea of replacement seems a logical means to avoid aging.

HORMONES: COMPARATIVE BIOLOGICAL RESEARCH

As intimated at the outset of this paper, the everyday cultural logic and models reflected in media and pop clinical views depict hormones, particularly testosterone, as causal agents that organize sex and sexuality. This attitude contrasts sharply with a substantial body of biological research. First, wide-ranging comparative studies have demonstrated that agency in sexual behavior is not intrinsic to hormones such as testosterone. Rather, evolved species-specific mechanisms are responsible for entraining behaviors to testicular activity, of which circulating testosterone is a good physiological index.

For instance, in studies of reproductive biology, David Crews and others have shown that in some taxa sexual behavior is dissociated from gonadal hormones in either or both sexes (Crews 1984; Crews and Moore 1986). Extensive studies in birds (reviewed in Wingfield et al. 1990) show the threshold of circulating T compatible with sperm production and sexual behavior to be rather low, and the wide range of T above this low threshold is associated with territoriality and male-male conflict during breeding season. The male-male aggression, however, driving raised T levels, also reduces male parental care, which is counterproductive if paternal care is important for offspring survival. Therefore, the degree to which T output is affected by behavioral cues such as male-male conflict correlates with the ratio of male conflict to paternal care in bird species. In men, biological and psychological stress, as well as subordination, acutely suppress T, but effects of stress and failure on

Table 1

Sex Differences in Total Burden of Disease by Source, Expressed in
Disability-Adjusted Life Years (DALYs) Lost to Morbidity and Mortality

Source	Total Burden in 10^5 DALYs	
	Males	Females
Perinatal	551.8	444.7
Communicable	2505.9	1830.0
Noncommunicable	2981.6	2772.8
Maternal	0.0	297.2
Injuries	1092.1	533.9

Source: World Bank Annual Report, 1993

sexual behavior occur largely through psychobehavioral routes only slightly affected by T levels.

There are good reasons why males minimize exposure to testosterone by dampening or curtailing its production whenever possible, as in seasonally breeding birds and primates, among whom the testes become inactive outside breeding season. Testosterone is an "expensive" hormone, a source for the "male disadvantage" in morbidity and mortality. In the case of humans, the androgen-induced disadvantage is considerable—with the exception of maternal burden, males bear a much greater health burden than do females (Table 1). Mortality reflects both biological vulnerability and environmental challenge, including risk behaviors and social factors. If one examines the sources of male health burden in terms of sex ratio of mortality by developmental period and relative contribution of biological-intrinsic and social causes, one finds that mortality from intrinsic causes is greater in males than in females at all ages. Risk-taking behavior, however, plays an increasing role in differential male mortality from childhood to adulthood.

Testosterone levels in adult men exceed those in women by at least ten- to twenty-fold. Such high levels not only confer reproductive and productive benefits but also incur maintenance and psychobehavioral costs (Table 2). Due to intratesticular sequestration of T, spermatogenesis is sustained at fairly low circulating levels and is scarcely perturbed

Carol M. Worthman

Table 2
Androgen Costs and Benefits in Males

PHYSICAL CHARACTERISTICS	BENEFITS
Spermatogenesis	[Obvious]
Sex Characteristics	Male-Male Competition, Female Choice
Libido	Mating Drive, Competence
Blood Chemistry	Increased Work Capacity

PHYSICAL CHARACTERISTICS	COSTS
Increased Muscle	Increased BMR, Maintenance Costs
Increased Size	Increased BMR, Maintenance Costs
Decreased Immune Function	Increased Morbidity and Mortality
Increased Physical "Wear"	Increased Aging, Decreased Life Expectancy

by acute fluctuation in that hormone. Testosterone generates and maintains secondary sex characters (e.g., beard growth and muscularity), and fluctuations in that hormone are linked to libido, stress, subordination, and other psychobehavioral patterns. Androgenization also is costly. Testosterone-induced developmental effects permanently increase maintenance costs for men. First, their prolonged growth and increased peak height velocity generate 5–10 percent greater body size than women. Second, anabolic effects of androgen induce muscle bulking and increase body proportion of this metabolically "expensive" tissue, especially compared to the energetically cheaper fat deposition promoted by estrogens in women. Sex differences in body composition generate sex differences in metabolic rate and underlie increased caloric need and nutritional vulnerability of men. Numerous other physiological effects of androgens, including those on blood chemistry, metabolism, immune function, and stress response, have been linked to accelerated physical damage in the adult years with concomitant risk for morbidity and mortality. Absence of breeding season in humans removes the possibility of periodic testicular dampening in men, which leaves them continuously exposed to high levels of androgen in adulthood.

Furthermore, recent findings suggest that our views of androgen and aging are simply ethnocentric, limited by data from the groups that have been studied, that is, well-nourished, epidemiologically privileged Western populations of the late twentieth century. Mounting evidence from non-Western populations suggests that androgen patterns in Westerners are unusual. Our first intimation of this bias came during our comparative studies of adolescent development, in which we noticed that the young people we were studying were clearly on different developmental trajectories for adrenal androgens than the ones published for Western clinical populations with which we were familiar.

For instance, we contrasted two New Guinea populations: the quite slowly maturing Hagahai, who were under pathogen and acculturative stress; and the more rapidly maturing Amele, who were relatively healthy and well nourished. Testosterone of young men ages twenty-one to twenty-five years in these groups differed markedly (Figure 1), with the Amele having nearly twice as much T as Hagahai; however, both tended to be lower than their American peers. This profile was even more dramatic for DHEAS, which peaks by age twenty-five. Peak values for both groups fall short even of those measured in thirteen-year-old boys in our large sample of American adolescents.

These and other studies in reproductive ecology raised the possibility that developmental-organizational processes can lead to population variation in endocrine regulation and output that reflect different life history trajectories. About three years ago we commenced lifespan endocrinologic studies to pursue those questions. On September 15, the day before publication of the *Newsweek* issue discussed above, we submitted abstracts of work with Cynthia Beall on two high-altitude agropastoralist populations in Bolivia and Tibet (Worthman, Beall, and Stallings 1997a, 1997b). The lifespan patterns we found in nominally healthy adults at all ages did not fit those expected from Western clinical literature.

The data on testosterone (Figure 1) contrasts visibly with the age-related declines reported for American men. Bolivian Aymara men over age twenty-five do not display strong quantitative declines in T, but T does negatively associate with age. By contrast, Tibetan men exhibited no association of T with age, and indeed on average appear to increase T through the sixth decade.

DHEAS, largely of adrenal origin, showed a similar pattern (Figure 2). Age-related decline is evident in Aymara men over age twenty-

Figure 1
Testosterone by Age in Men of Three Populations, in Bolivia, Tibet, and the U.S.

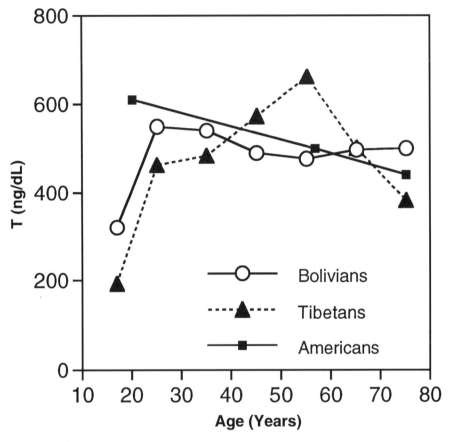

Source for Bolivia and Tibet: Worthman, Beall, and Stallings 1997a; for U.S.: Gray et al. 1991

five. Tibetan men, by contrast, failed to show such decreases. The population differences in age-related trends leads to significant divergence in their mean values by the fifth decade. Even more striking than the disparity in profiles of DHEAS by age in these two populations is the comparison of both with concentrations in Westerners. American men in their early twenties have double the average concentration of DHEAS of their counterparts in either of our non-Western study groups. Moreover, American men experience a 3.0 percent annual decline in DHEAS

Figure 2
DHEAS by Age in Men of Three Populations, in Bolivia, Tibet, and the U.S.

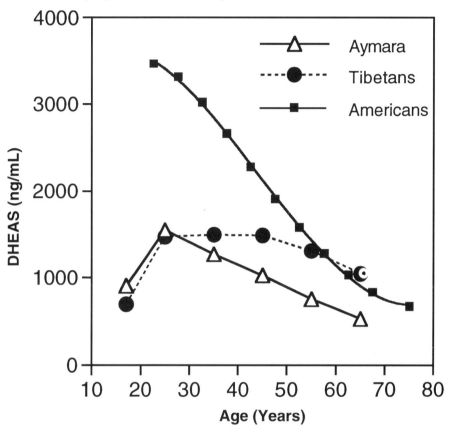

Source for Bolivia and Tibet: Worthman, Beall, and Stallings 1997b; for the U.S.: Barrett-Conner, Khaw, and Yen 1986; Orentreich et al. 1984; Salvini et al. 1992.

after age twenty-five, whereas decreases in Bolivians are 1.0 percent per annum, and the lack of aging decreases in Tibetans leads to equivalent values for Americans and Tibetans by the sixth decade. The contrast in absolute values is not as great for T, but Americans alone have significant age-related declines.

These data demonstrate that: (1) populations differ in lifespan concentrations and trajectories of T, and, particularly, DHEAS; (2) declining T or DHEAS is not an absolute concomitant of aging; and (3) absence of a decrease in T or DHEAS does not prevent aging (i.e., Tibetan men do not live longer than Americans). Therefore, it is premature to conclude that falling concentrations of these hormones cause aging, rather than the converse, and that maintenance of androgens with hormone replacement will forestall aging.

We do not know whether, across the range of variation in androgen levels reported here, absolute differences in T or DHEAS have significant implications for function or health. Nor do we know the significance of variation in rates of change. Does having more of either hormone correlate with better sexual or reproductive function or faithfully reflect a better state of health? In the case of testosterone, we do know that men's sexual behavior, libido, and fertility are uncorrelated with tonic T across a wide range of values, and are related only at the ends of the distribution.

In summary, our current knowledge of both comparative and human biology refutes, on at least three counts, the popular views linking androgens, particularly testosterone, to men's sexuality, longevity, and youthfulness. First, organization of sexual behavior is not intrinsic to androgens, and humans may be said to show a weakly associated pattern of hormone-behavior relationship. Second, androgens, or rather the biobehavioral reproductive efforts they organize, are metabolically and behaviorally expensive, a reality reflected in adaptations by males of many vertebrate species to dampen testicular function outside breeding periods, or, in the case of humans and some other primates, decrease their output during periods of stress such as illness, hunger, or fear and subordination. Perhaps androgen output is up-regulated in Americans because their consistently favorable conditions inform their bodies that they can "afford" to do so regardless of cost. On the other hand, it may be that highly competitive social settings, combined with such permissive conditions, drive elevated androgens (Wingfield et al. 1990). Third, study of Americans may not provide a full picture of human potential in endocrine function or of aging processes. Populations differ in absolute concentrations of androgens of testicular and adrenal origin, as well as in trajectories of these hormones with age. The biological significance of such differences is unknown, as are the relative costs and benefits of absolute differences or relative change in circulating T or DHEAS concentrations. Moreover, psychobiological and behavioral as well as biological costs and benefits need to be considered, for there is more to sexuality or health than simple physical integrity.

TOWARD A BIOCULTURAL PERSPECTIVE

There is much we could discuss about the data and the concepts this biological analysis has raised, including life history theory and the possibility of endocrine involvement in facultative adaptation in life history organization. For now, however, let us return briefly to our starting point, the consideration of American cultural constructions of biology as reflected in views of men's sexuality and aging.

First, it seems that anthropology can teach us the same lesson about human biology that it does about culture. That is, only by probing the full range of human conditions can we obtain a more representative picture of what it is to be human. Comparative lifespan endocrinology shows that the biology of aging presented in much of the clinical literature and reflected in the *Newsweek* article is ethnocentric, limited to populations representing a narrow ecological and temporal range of human experience. There may not be "a" biology of sexuality and aging, but rather many such biologies across a range of human social and physical ecologies. This does not mean that we may not determine that different biological states reflect different states of function or well-being, or that we may not therefore assign a hierarchy of desirable biological statuses based on our evaluation of costs and benefits. A comparative approach, however, opens the way for such evaluation. It leads us to question whether our views of what is "natural" are actually local and culture-specific.

Second, the mere fact that views of biology are grounded in culture does not mean that they have no biological salience. Insofar as cultural models inform behavior, they inform human ecology and have deep biological implications for domains such as human sexuality and aging. Consider, for instance, the image from the cover of a publication from the major retirement fund for educators in the United States, in which a yellow and black neoprene-suited elderly man, pelvis cocked, "Intensity" emblazoned on his thigh, is apparently waterskiing while holding the tow rope in his teeth. He is a product of a life history course defined by low morbidity and mortality, consistently excellent nutrition, consequent early maturation, and low subsistence wear or energetic demands. These hard-won, culturally valued circumstances also reflect deep aspects of social organization and resource allocation. They have dramatically increased the probability of his survival to this age, and they have imprinted the regulatory and functional systems of the body. A high cultural value is also placed on performance and on sexuality, which are equated for men. There is, moreover, a mapping of sports metaphors of performance—faster, farther, higher—onto definitions of competence and therefore of self. These factors propel the man in the brochure into that suit and onto those skis.

What does it say of the self and of our cultural constructions of life history that the brochure cover depicting the waterskier bears the over-script "Born to Retire"? The juvenilization of elderhood as an extension of young adulthood may occur because our views of old age are incompatible with our gendered and performative values defining selfhood. Indeed, elderhood is rapidly becoming pathologized, and the threshold for elderhood is declining to middle age through the reification and pathologization of "menopause" and "viropause." Such cultural logic also leads to a high demand for androgen replacement to maintain performance by sustaining the mental and physical sexual attributes of youth, a developmental truncation eschewing or rejecting progression to further life course outcomes. This logic also fuels dieting, exercising, self-help preoccupation, and a host of other decisions about time and resource allocation that influence individual psychological and physical well-being and further fuel cultural constructions of the life course as well as economic and sociopolitical structural conditions.

To conclude, as a member of a sex that has struggled against the commercialization of the body, the confusion of self with appearance, the conflation of self with biological status, the co-optation of one's well-being by experts, and the moral economy that underlies all of these factors, I should alert men to an emerging, familiar cultural logic represented in the closing lines of the *Newsweek* piece: "The sad truth is that staying manly takes more than money. It takes work" (Cowley 1996: 75). The moral economy of "faster, farther, higher" may extend poorly into the cultural work of constructing meaningful experiences of aging and elderhood—and it may not work too well for other parts of the lifespan, either. Part of the "work of culture" must be individual construction of a sustainable, meaningful life course. If our society is to achieve that work of culture and accommodate human needs across the expanded range of life expectancy that some aspects of our culture have gained for us, then we need a similarly expanded view of human biology and of self. I hope to have conveyed here some sense of how comparative biocultural analyses can be a productive way of exploring those issues.

REFERENCES

Barrett-Connor, E., K-T Khaw, and S. S. C. Yen. 1986. A Prospective Study of Dehydroepiandrosterone Sulfate, Mortality, and Cardiovascular Disease. *New England Journal of Medicine* 315:1519–24.

Cowley, G. 1996. Attention: Aging Men. *Newsweek*, September 16, 68–75.

Crews, D. 1984. Gamete Production, Sex Hormone Secretion, and Mating Behavior Uncoupled. *Hormones and Behavior* 18:22–28.

Crews, D., and M. C. Moore. 1986. Evolution of Mechanisms Controlling Mating Behavior. *Science* 231:121–25.

Gray, A., J. A. Berlin, J. B. McKinlay, and C. Longcope. 1991. Examination of Research Design Effects on the Association of Testosterone and Male Aging: Results of a Meta-Analysis. *Journal of Clinical Epidemiology* 44:671–84.

Orentreich, N., J. L. Brind, R. L. Rizer, and J. H. Vogelman. 1984. Age Changes and Sex Differences in Serum Dehydroepiandrosterone Sulfate Concentrations Throughout Adulthood. *Journal of Clinical Endocrinology and Metabolism* 59:551–55.

Salvini, S., M. J. Stampfer, R. L. Barbieri, and C. H. Hennekens. 1992. Effects of Age, Smoking, and Vitamins on Plasma DHEAS Levels: A Cross-Sectional Study in Men. *Journal of Clinical Epidemiology* 74:139–43.

Wingfield, J. C., R. E. Hegner, A. M. Duffy, and G. F. Fall. 1990. The "Challenge Hypothesis": Theoretical Implications for Patterns of Testosterone Secretion, Mating Systems, and Breeding Strategies. *American Naturalist* 136:829–46.

World Bank. 1993. *World Development Report*. New York: Oxford University Press.

Worthman, C. M., C. M. Beall, and J. F. Stallings. 1997a. Population Variation in Reproductive Function of Men. *American Journal of Physical Anthropology*, suppl. 24:246.

———. 1997b. Population Differences in DHEAS Across the Lifespan: Implications for Aging. *American Journal of Human Biology* 9(1):149.

Human Sexual Behavior and Evolution

Linda D. Wolfe

As a result of millions of years of evolution, the biological basis of human sexuality is shared with other animals. This essay considers those long-term evolutionary events that formed the basic reproductive biology of primates, including humans. With the evolution of modern humans, mating behavior came to be shaped by culture. In other words, there is a biological dimension to human sexual behavior, and sex and gender among humans are largely informed by culture.

With regard to the biological dimension of our sexuality, it is worth asking, What are the biological characteristics of reproduction in our species? Like other mammals, we are limited to sexual reproduction — that is, reproduction accomplished by the coming together of sexed haploid gametes (i.e., ova and sperm) produced by the process of meiosis. Sexed gametes are in turn produced by sexed adults who make either ova or sperm throughout their adult lives. Many nonmammalian species are more varied and less limited in their mode of reproduction than are mammals.

Other mammalian traits that typify humans include internal fertilization, live birth, and the suckling of neonates. Humans are also characterized by spontaneous but at least partially concealed ovulation, a menstrual cycle, and a set of hormones and pheromones that may help coordinate female desire and ovulation, and sexually motivate males. The events that produced the reproductive biology of our species are part of the interesting tale of the twists and turns of the evolution of life on our planet.

SEXUAL REPRODUCTION

The first major innovation in the way animals reproduce occurred about two billion years ago with the evolution of single-celled eukaryote plants and animals, which were the first cells to reproduce by meiosis, that is, to reproduce sexually (Dyer and Obar 1994). Eukaryote cells have two sets of chromosomes and must, therefore, undergo meiosis. In other words, they must halve the number of chromosomes in the germ cell or gamete before reproduction can occur. There are, of course, advantages and disadvantages to sexual reproduction. While it is not clear that sexual reproduction has *more* advantages than asexual reproduction, two often-cited advantages that it does have are increases in genetic variation, which facilitates adaptation to novel environments; and restoration of damaged DNA (Michod 1995).

The earliest eukaryote cells, although reproducing sexually, perhaps did not have sexes; that is, all gametes were probably equal in size and mobility. On the other hand, anisogamy (i.e., having gametes of unequal size and mobility) is widespread among animals, including mammals. What, then, is the adaptive significance of sexed gametes; that is, why did ova and sperm evolve? The speculation is that ova and sperm are more efficient than same-sized gametes in that the relatively stationary ova specialized in carrying and conserving nutrients for a zygote, and sperm became equipped with the mobility to locate the ova. The specialization of the ova and sperm is perhaps the oldest form of division of labor by sex. Female choice of a mate (also referred to as "mate choice" or "sperm competition") is defined as that set of techniques that serve to thwart the attempts of other males to impregnate the ova of the female of their choosing. This procedure likely evolved concurrently with the evolution of sexed gametes (Michod 1995). Sexual reproduction involving the production of ova and sperm by sexed adults probably evolved with the earliest vertebrates, perhaps as early as 600 million years ago (Carroll 1988; Jefferies 1986).

Internal Fertilization

Internal fertilization evolved later, when the first reptiles laid eggs and adapted to living and reproducing on land about 350 million years ago (Martin and Sumida 1997). Building on the reptilian adaptations, mammals as we think of them—that is, animals with placentas, live births, and postnatal nursing of offspring—likely evolved some time after 140 million years ago but before 65 million years ago (Strickberger 1996; Kielan-Jaworowska, Brown, and Lillegraven 1979).

Retaining the fetus in the uterus of the female and the innovation of the placenta perhaps evolved as adaptations to a cold climate and/or as a way to protect the fetus from predation. The basic biological system supporting reproduction among mammals was likely well in place by 65 million years ago, at the beginning of the mammalian radiation. In short, the basic biological system of mammals included sexual reproduction involving ova and sperm produced by permanently sexed adults, internal fertilization, live birth that necessitated the placenta and postnatal nursing of offspring, and a hormonal and pheromonal system to coordinate ovulation, female sexual desire, and male mounting behavior.

Primates

The first true primates are currently believed to have evolved around 60 million years ago (Covert 1997). The sexual behavior and physiology of these early primates probably followed the typical mammalian pattern already described. Martin (1975) discussed the observation that for many prosimians the vagina is closed except during ovulation and suggests that this feature may be the ancestral primate condition. According to Martin, this periodic closure of the vagina indicates a seasonal breeding system (as found in many prosimians) or a long-phase ovulatory cycle rather than a year-round breeding system or a short-phase ovulatory cycle. In other words, mating would have been confined to a few days each year and would have been geared to the photoperiodicity of the earth and local environmental conditions.

Catarrhine Primates

By about 35 million years ago, catarrhines (i.e., Old World primates) appear in the fossil record (Kay, Ross, and Williams 1997). For reasons that are currently unclear but probably relate to increases in brain size and the evolution of compulsive sociality, the biology of reproduction seems to have undergone changes in the last common ancestor of the catarrhine primates. The female catarrhine pattern of reproductive biology is that of continuous sexual receptivity, a short-phase ovulatory cycle, and a vagina that is open throughout the reproductive cycle.

Estrus in allocatarrhine primates (i.e., Old World primates other than humans) is often confused with estrus in other mammals. Estrus in mammals, including primates, as it is currently understood, has three components: attractivity, proceptivity, and receptivity. Attractivity is defined as a female's effectiveness at sexually stimulating a male. Proceptivity comprises the sexual appetitive behaviors of a female. Receptivity is those female reactions that facilitate a fertile copulation with a male (Beach 1976). In primates estrogen has been associated with attractivity and proceptivity. The role of androgens in proceptivity is unclear at this time. Progesterone tends to inhibit proceptivity. (For further discussion see Wolfe 1991.)

With regard to behavior, allocatarrhine females are receptive to male mounting throughout the menstrual cycle and even during pregnancy. In other words, engaging in sexual intercourse for female allocatarrhines is less dependent on the timing of ovulation and hormones than in other mammals, and more often shaped by social cues. No hormones are associated with receptivity—even ovariectomized allocatarrhine females remain sexually receptive (Johnson and Phoenix 1976). Estrus in allocatarrhine primates is not, therefore, to be defined as sexual receptivity, as it often is in other mammals. Estrus in monkeys and apes is more accurately defined as that time period when the female engages in proceptive behavior or "sexually appetitive behavior directed by a female toward a male" (Nadler 1992:194). Proceptive behavior may or may not correlate with ovulation, depending on the individual female and her social situation.

In those allocatarrhine species with a midcycle swelling of the genital area associated with ovulation (a "sex swelling"), mating is more closely timed to ovulation than it is in those species who lack the sex swelling. The correlation between the sex swelling and sexual behavior is not with female receptivity but with attractivity. That is, males are more attracted to females with a sex swelling than to those who are not swollen. Chimpanzees and about half of the Old World monkey species have a sex swelling (Wolfe 1991). It is likely that the sex swelling evolved independently in the chimpanzee and Old World monkey lineages. The human lineage, like that of the gorilla and orangutan, did not evolve a sex swelling, nor did the human lineage have an ancestor with a sex swelling (Gray and Wolfe 1983). Among those allocatarrhine species without the sex swelling, ovulation is anatomically concealed, although allocatarrhine females may behave more proceptively at the time of ovulation. On the other hand, proceptive behavior cannot necessarily be taken as an indicator of ovulation in any of the allocatarrhine females (Hrdy 1995).

Concealed Ovulation

The question remains, however, whether ovulation in modern humans is completely concealed. That is, is there evidence that women have the typical allocatarrhine pattern of continuous sexual receptivity throughout the menstrual cycle with fluctuations in proceptive behaviors and attractiveness associated with ovulation? Although the literature is somewhat contradictory, there is some evidence that women are similar to other catarrhine females. For example, an experiment conducted by Hill and Wenzel (1981) suggests that hormonal changes may influence a woman's attractivity. They found that men at a nightclub were more likely to touch women who were midcycle than they were to touch women at other phases of their monthly cycle. Adams, Gold, and Burt (1978) found that married women exhibited elevated frequencies of both autosexual and female-initiated heterosexual behavior at midcycle. A research project by Matteo and Rissman (1984:250) involving lesbians living in stable pairs also found that "women, like other female mammals, show more proceptive behaviors or may be more attractive at midcycle." While the evidence is equivocal, it suggests that ovulation is not completely concealed in humans (Wood 1994).

Orgasm

Is orgasm unique to human females, or is it also part of the experience of other primates? Anthropologists have assumed that the female orgasm is unique to humans and have built models of human evolution based on that assumption. Though not an anthropologist, Robert Ardrey did express ideas gathered from the anthropological literature. His statement (1976:88–89) on the female orgasm typifies much of the literature on human evolution:

> The capacity [for female orgasm] varies so widely among individuals that one must suspect a very recent evolutionary heritage. . . .
> The female's varying is so remarkable, one must suspect that it is fairly new in evolutionary terms and so is subject to the inhibitions

of culture. But this we may suspect: the female orgasm through enhancement of female desire provided one further guarantee that the males would return from the hunt. The male might be tired: female desire would refresh him. The male's orgasm, perfected through the ages, is a reflex: the female's demands a certain discipline, a concentration on the part of the central nervous system. I should doubt very much that female reward preceded by long the enlargement of the great human brain.

There was, however, never any actual evidence that other primate females did not experience orgasm. I would, in fact, argue the opposite: there is evidence that monkey and ape females do experience orgasm and may actually have an easier time of it than women.

Observations during sexual stimulation of Old World monkeys and apes (including clutching reactions, facial expressions, vocalizations, contractions of perineal muscles, uterine contractions, and changes in breathing and pulse rates during sexual intercourse) all suggest that monkey and ape females do indeed experience orgasm (Burton 1971). If we compare the genital anatomy of the allocatarrhines with that of women, we see that there are differences that might explain some of the difficulties women have in attaining orgasm when the only stimulation is that of sexual intercourse. In the allocatarrhine female, the urinary meatus is found either inside the vagina or near the base of the vagina (Eckstein 1958). The clitoris, in turn, is also found near the base of the vagina, and in some allocatarrhines, such as the chimpanzee, it may be relatively larger than the human clitoris (Graham and Bradley 1972). Because of the location of the clitoris in allocatarrhine females, it is likely that it receives direct stimulation during intercourse, an action that would, of course, facilitate orgasm. Human females, on the other hand, have the urinary meatus located in the vulva between the vagina and the clitoris. In other words, the clitoris is located away from the base of the vagina. The most likely explanation for the genital anatomy of women is that as the size of the neonatal head increased about 750,000 years ago there was selection to move the urinary meatus away from the base of the vagina to protect it from trauma during childbirth. Because the clitoris is located away from the base of the vagina, it does not receive direct stimulation during sexual intercourse, thereby contributing to the difficulties women often have attaining orgasm when stimulation is limited to sexual intercourse. When women receive direct stimulation of the clitoris, they attain orgasm in about the same time period as men (Fisher 1973). At the present time, I believe we have to conclude that orgasm is part of the female allocatarrhine reaction to sexual stimulation and not a unique feature of the sexual behavior of women.

Homosexual Behavior

Vasey published the first review article on primate homosexual behavior and reported that "this behavior is phylogenetically widespread among higher primates, but totally absent among the lemurs. The majority of the 33 species that demonstrate homosexual behavior do so rarely, but for a substantial number (N = 12) it appears to be a more common pattern under free-ranging conditions" (Vasey 1995:173).

The full extent to which primates engage in homosexual behavior is unknown, because these behaviors have not been consistently reported. I think we can infer, however, that for many primates, homosexual interactions are part of the total repertoire of sexual behavior. As more primatologists publish their observations on the full range of the sexual behaviors of the animals they study, a more comprehensive view of primate sexual behavior will emerge.

DISCUSSION

The evidence indicates that humans are not unlike the other catarrhine primates in their reproductive behaviors. In fact, I would argue that we are fairly average catarrhines in that regard. As a result of millions of years of evolution, our reproductive biology is based on sexed, haploid gametes produced by permanently sexed adults, spontaneous ovulation, and a set of hormones that coordinate ovulation, the proceptive behaviors of women, and mating interest of men. Boys and girls, like juvenile allocatarrhines, spend much of their time playing and practicing adult roles. After puberty young males and females inform potential partners of their willingness to mate through courtship and approach patterns. Offspring eventually result from mating, and the cycle begins again. Ovulation in humans is at least partially concealed, as it is in the Old World monkeys and apes who lack a sex swelling. While orgasm is a possibility for humans and the allocatarrhine females, the anatomy of women prevents direct stimulation of the clitoris during sexual inter-course, thereby making it somewhat difficult to attain orgasm. Homo-sexual and heterosexual interactions characterize both humans and many Old World monkeys and apes.

On the other hand, the adage "Sex always means" aptly describes only our species. That is, humans, with their capacity for language and myth-making, symbolize sex so that all sexual interactions, no matter how brief, are embedded in cultural meanings—meanings about sex with or without marriage, adultery, sexuality, gender relationships, how people give and receive pleasure, beauty, genital mutilation, and so on. Moreover, much of human social organization and mythologizing is re-lated to the fact that humans are permanently sexed mammals. Having permanently sexed individuals allows for the construction of gender and the assigning of appropriate behaviors for each gender. Human society would be very different if it were not organized around gender and the roles and obligations of gender, and if each person had an equal chance of becoming pregnant. Human sexual dimorphism in body size is prob-ably at least partially the result of sexual selection that is, of course, re-lated to the circumstance of being a permanently sexed species. The fea-tures of human behavior, however, that are not directly related to gender, such as greed, jealousy, peace and reconciliation, warfare, and the con-stant maneuvering for position and status, would not necessarily be dif-ferent. The differences between ourselves and the other primates are not so much in the underlying biology of reproduction or in actual mating behaviors but in the cultural meanings humans attach to their sexuality and sexual behaviors.

REFERENCES

Adams, D. B., A. R. Gold, and A. D. Burt. 1978. Rise in Female-Initiated Sex-ual Activity at Ovulation and Its Suppression by Oral Contraceptives. *New England Journal of Medicine* 299:1145–50.

Ardrey, R. 1976. *The Hunting Hypothesis*. New York: Atheneum.

Beach, F. A. 1976. Sexual Attractivity, Proceptivity, and Receptivity in Female Mammals. *Hormones and Behavior* 7:105–38.

Burton, F. D. 1971. Sexual Climax in Female *Macaca mulatta*. In *Proceedings of the Third International Congress of Primatology*, ed. F. D. Burton, pp. 180–91. Basel: Karger.

Carroll, R. L. 1988. *Vertebrate Paleontology and Evolution*. New York: W. H. Freeman.

Covert, H. H. 1997. The Early Primate Adaptive Radiation and New Evidence About Anthropoid Origins. In *Biological Anthropology: The State of the Science*, 2d ed., ed. N. T. Boaz and L. D. Wolfe, pp. 1–23. Bend, Ore.: IIHER.

Dyer, B. D., and R. A. Obar. 1994. *Tracing the History of Eukaryotic Cells*. New York: Columbia University Press.

Eckstein, P. 1958. Internal Reproductive Organs. In *Primatologia*, ed. H. Hofer, A. H. Schultz, and D. Starck, pp. 542–620. Basel: Karger.

Fisher, S. 1973. *The Female Orgasm*. New York: Basic Books.

Graham, C. E., and C. F. Bradley. 1972. Microanatomy of Chimpanzee Genital System. In *The Chimpanzee: Histology, Reproduction, and Restraint*, ed. G. H. Bourne, pp. 77–126. Baltimore: University Park Press.

Gray, J. P., and L. D. Wolfe. 1983. Human Female Sexual Cycles and the Concealment of Ovulation Problem. *Journal of Social and Biological Structures* 6:345–52.

Hill, E. M., and P. A. Wenzel. 1981. Variation in Ornamentation and Behavior in a Discotheque for Females Observed at Differing Menstrual Phases. Paper presented at the annual meeting of the Animal Behavior Society.

Hrdy, S. B. 1995. The Primate Origins of Female Sexuality and Their Implications for Nonconceptive Sex in the Reproductive Strategies of Women. *Human Evolution* 10:131–44.

Jefferies, R. P. S. 1986. *The Ancestry of the Vertebrates*. London: Cambridge University Press.

Johnson, D. F., and C. H. Phoenix. 1976. Hormonal Control of Female Sexual Attractiveness, Proceptivity, and Receptivity in Rhesus Monkeys. *Journal of Comparative and Physiological Psychology* 90:473–83.

Kay, R. F., C. Ross, and B. A. Williams. 1997. Anthropoid Origins. *Science* 275:797–804.

Kielan-Jaworowska, Z., T. M. Brown, and J. A. Lillegraven. 1979. Eutheria. In *Mesozoic Mammals: The First Two-Thirds of Mammalian History*, ed. J. A. Lillegraven, Z. Kielan-Jaworowska, and W. A. Clemens, pp. 221–58. Berkeley and Los Angeles: University of California Press.

Martin, K. L. M., and S. S. Sumida. 1997. An Integrated Approach to the Origin of Amniotes: Completing the Transition to Land. In *Amniote Origins: Completing the Transition to Land*, ed. S. S. Sumida and K. L. M. Martin, pp. 1–8. San Diego: Academic Press.

Martin, R. D. 1975. The Bearing of Reproductive Behavior and Ontogeny on Strepsirhine Phylogeny. In *Phylogeny of the Primate*, ed. W. P. Luckett and F. S. Szalay, pp. 265–97. New York: Plenum Press.

Matteo, S., and E. F. Rissman. 1984. Increased Sexual Activity During the Midcycle Portion of the Human Menstrual Cycle. *Hormones and Behavior* 18:249–55.

Michod, R. E. 1995. *Eros and Evolution: A Natural Philosophy of Sex.* Reading, Mass.: Helix Books.

Nadler, R. D. 1992. Sexual Behavior and the Concept of Estrus in the Great Apes. In *Topics in Primatology*, vol. 2, ed. N. Itoigawa, Y. Sugiyama, G. P. Sackett, and R. K. R. Thompson, pp. 191–208. Tokyo: University of Tokyo Press.

Strickberger, M. W. 1996. *Evolution*, 2d ed. Boston: Jones and Bartlett.

Vasey, P. 1995. Homosexual Behavior in Primates: A Review of Evidence and Theory. *International Journal of Primatology* 16:173–204.

Wolfe, L. D. 1991. Human Evolution and the Sexual Behavior of Female Primates. In *Understanding Behavior*, ed. J. D. Loy and C. B. Peters, pp. 121–51. New York: Oxford University Press.

Wood, J. W. 1994. *Dynamics of Human Reproduction: Biology, Biometry, Demography*. New York: Aldine de Gruyter.

A Discussion of Culture, Biology, and Sexuality: Toward Synthesis

Ernestine Friedl

These papers on the anthropological study of sexuality, taken together, eloquently present us with the dilemmas facing anthropology at the turn of the twenty-first century. Sexuality as a focus enables us to consider the purposes for anthropological study in general, the conscious and unconscious theoretical propositions that guide our work, the issues subsuming participant observation, and the writing of ethnography. Sexuality is a particularly poignant topic, for it returns us to the holistic concerns of anthropology as a study of humans as biological and cultural animals organized into societies.

Anthropologists have heretofore concentrated on the objects of sexual activity, on the persons and activities thought to be appropriate and inappropriate for sexual congress in a wide range of societies. We are familiar with the endless discussions of the incest taboo, of adolescent freedom or restraint, of sexual acts as relations of power and as part of ritual, of sexual symbolism in religion and art. All the contexts subsume the existence of sexuality as part of the human essence and thereby subject to regulation and control, to cultural, social, and psychological constructions. The virtue of these collected papers is that the authors are concerned with just what that assumed sexuality is and how understanding can contribute to the anthropological enterprise. The title of this volume tells us that the authors have analyzed sexuality as both cultural and biological and have attempted a synthesis.

Wolfe's paper takes us directly into human evolutionary considerations. The study of nonhuman primate sexualities provides insight but not models for possibilities in *Homo sapiens* sexuality.

Suggs and Miracle believe that we have been prevented from fusing biology and culture by our underlying theoretical stances. We have too often separated materialistic approaches from structural ones and sociobiology from postmodernism. They want to interpret the particular *and* explain the general. They consider cultural materialism still the most fruitful theoretical stance, but only if it is revised to counteract its current deficiencies. The theory has neglected the relationship between the individual and society, and especially the significance of individual agency. It also fails to explain the continuity of ideas and symbols in the face of infrastructural change. Sexuality as a locus of investigation might become a source of significant revision.

Frayser and Herdt have helped us understand why sexuality has been so rarely studied by European anthropologists, who, as we know, are not exempt from the taboos of their own cultures. The separation of body and soul and the sense that the body is dirty have kept anthropologists and nonanthropologists alike embarrassed by the topic. It is noteworthy that Sherry Ortner, in a well-known paper, develops the analogy that male is to culture as female is to nature. She explains female assignment to nature as based on women's handling of the bodily fluids associated with infants. Sexual acts are, by definition and as the papers have indicated, private. Moreover, a strong sense of personal privacy also prevents easy conversation about sex. We now stress the importance of the positionality of the ethnographer as an influence on field observations. There has been an increase in European societies of sexually explicit and bawdy conversation and images, particularly among women and the young. There is also a search for political power and social acceptance in the homosexual community. As Herdt remarks, the AIDS phenomenon has been added to these trends to relieve some of the unease about explicitly sexual study.

Positionality also leads to the analysis of the culture of the ethnographer in relation to the people in the study. There is a considerable body of literature on the advantages and disadvantages of doing ethnography in one's own cultural group. Gender considerations are also germane to that discussion. Do homosexual and lesbian ethnographers have an advantage over others in studying sexuality, including homosexual practices, as women are said to have in studying women, or African Americans in studying African American communities, or Greeks studying

Greeks? And if there is an advantage, what is it? And what sensitivities are gained or lost? In my view, they probably balance out.

Worthman has provided us with a fascinating illustration of how sexual studies can make major contributions to the biology and culture nexus. American emphasis on youth and its sexual prowess, along with our assumption that everything can be fixed by technology, is also fueled by folk assumptions that sex is in the hormones. It has been discovered that the decrease in the production of androgens with advancing age is not panhuman, but can vary among people in different settings. This very important datum confirms the finding that testosterone levels interact with social, cultural, and biological circumstances of a given situation and are not necessarily the primary causal element in masculinity. But even more important, Worthman's counterintuitive discoveries lead to questions about whether and under what circumstances symbolic and incomplete folk understandings can change in the face of what we define as rationally collected information.

Jankowiak reminds us of the importance of factoring love, intimacy, tenderness, and affection into our understanding of human relations. It is rarely noted that sexuality includes these elements in addition to biological functioning. Such sentiments have cultural forms, and they influence sexual as well as all social relations. He also joins in the discussion of how scholars can deal with the invisibility of sex, with the evidence that it is almost always a private act invisible to others. It is only what people say about it that we can study—perhaps we can deal with some rituals and pornography, but the symbolic cannot be related to or tested by observation. Statements about sexual behavior, more than those dealing with most spheres of life, may be nonpredictive of actual behavior, of practice, because it is a secret act and can encompass a variety of behaviors. Ethnographers can, of course, engage in sex with the local people, but what ethical problems such behavior raises!

This circumstance adds to Frayser's concern with the overemphasis on the particular, without looking at similarities that make comparison possible. Without comparison anthropology loses its claim to trying to understand the human condition. I share Frayser's view that anthropology then produces a thing of shreds and patches, aesthetically pleasing but intellectually sterile.

Herdt asks the question, How could we put sexual study in relation to political and social study? Gender analysis certainly needs to be combined with sexuality and sexual behavior. How flexible *is* gender identity? How does it vary culturally? Herdt also asks to what aspects of culture gender and sexuality are *not* relevant. How well do anthropologists deal with emotionally and politically charged facets of human life? He also raises the special problems of getting informed consent in attempting to study sexuality.

What is the power of sexuality in the lives of a human's personal, social, political, and affective life? How do concepts of sexuality impinge on religious beliefs and practices, on children, kinship relations, political relations, and, of course, gender relations? The study is just beginning. The papers in this volume speed the enterprise on its way.

Appendix: Sex the Invisible

Ernestine Friedl

When your mind is set on mating
It is highly irritating
to see an ornithologist below:
Though it may be nature study,
To a bird it's merely bloody
Awful manners. Can't he see that he's *de trop*!

A. N. L. Munby, "Bird Watching"

After a quarter of a century of documenting and insisting on the importance of the cultural construction of gender and its inextricable relation
to time, history, and place, I find myself, as a materialist feminist, wanting to shift perspective in an attempt to add another dimension to the understanding of gender. The new perspective for me is to examine a panhuman custom, one that might have consequences for human gender
relations without reference to any particular culture or its history and
context.[1] It raises an old anthropological question: What is the nature of
human nature as reflected in human sexuality? The custom in question
is the human preference for conducting sexual intercourse, heterosexual
or homosexual, in private, invisible to all but the participants (and not
always visible even to them). We are all aware of the fascination, em-
barrassment, and prurience with which people, in zoos and on television, watch animals openly engage in coitus visible to both human
spectators and surrounding animals. We are uncomfortable because, in
human terms, we are unwittingly forced into voyeurism and even invol-
untary arousal. Ordinarily, run-of-the-mill, everyday sex relations in
virtually all human societies are hidden, conducted away from the gaze
of all but the participants.[2]

There are some exceptions in the ethnographic and historical literature, but they are so few that hidden coitus may safely be declared a near universal.[3] This holds true in spite of certain culturally defined special circumstances that may require or permit open rather than concealed sex acts. For example, in the United States houses of prostitution, homosexual bath houses, parties that turn into orgies, private sex clubs, and, of course, pornographic pictures and films are situations where the rule is suspended (Smith and Lynn 1970:284). For the purpose of providing a scientific study of sexual intercourse, Masters and Johnson asked volunteers to have sex in front of cameras while physiologic parameters were measured and recorded. Although gang rape is an aggressive act that uses sex as the medium of expression, it is visible sex to the participants. In some societies religious ceremonies and rituals may also prescribe that sex be conducted under the gaze of spectators. The power, potency, fascination, and titillation that infuse visible sex are forceful and effective precisely because the "normal" presumption of sexual privacy is being violated (Reiss 1986:33). In the same way, invisibility may enhance the pleasure of the act precisely because it is hidden.

However much it is prized, sexual privacy may be difficult to accomplish. When sex partners and children share sleeping spaces, the convention is to postpone sexual activity until children are not around or asleep. But if the children should wake or appear inopportunely, they are expected to act as if they saw nothing (Davenport 1977:150; Lee 1979: 461). In any case, sexual encounters are frequently enacted in the dark, and often under covers, so that lovemaking and coitus will not be visible to onlookers. Sounds may signal that intercourse is taking place, but who the participants are and what form the act takes generally remain invisible. When more than one sexually active couple occupy the same space without partitions (not an uncommon situation in the world's societies), the convention is that no one will watch. Symbolic seclusion through civil inattention reigns when actual privacy cannot be managed. To declare that sex acts are ordinarily hidden from view is hardly startling; it is common knowledge. The near universality of such behavior, however, is not well known. For example, the medieval historian James Brundage (1987:6) wrote: "As part of our medieval heritage, most of us still retain a deeply ingrained belief that sex is shameful and the respectable people should conduct their sexual activities in private, hidden

in the dark. These attitudes and beliefs are largely consequences of pa-
tristic and early medieval religious teachings holding that sex as a
source of moral defilement, spiritual pollution, and ritual impurity."
Brundage appears to be unaware that concealed sex is ubiquitous and
that it is practiced among many peoples who extol the pleasures of sex
and have none of the Christian view that it is defiling. As for the Christian world, it is not only "respectable people" who are expected to behave circumspectly.

In anthropological scholarship invisible sex comes into view as a special study in the reconstruction of the evolution of hominids. When I
first became intrigued with the subject of invisible sex in the early seventies and eighties, I found that a number of general works on the human animal did not even mention concealed sex as part of the human
condition (Alland 1972; Fisher 1982). That is no longer the case, and recently, Donald Brown, in a book devoted to human universals, included
concealed sex among his near universals (1991:39).[4] However, even
when it is mentioned, discussion is not extensive and treatment is often
perfunctory. For example, in his book *The Evolution of Human Sexuality*, Donald Symons relegates to a footnote his comment that privacy is
the outcome of reproductive competition. Having stated that it is not
feasible to copulate with all the partners with whom one might want to,
he continues (1979:67): "Humans are unprecedented among animals in
the subtlety with which they control and manipulate each others [*sic*]
sexuality, and it is often adaptive to keep sexual activities secret. The
seeking of privacy for sex probably has been uniformly adaptive and
hence is virtually universal among humans." These remarks do not constitute an explanation but are simply an assertion reminiscent of functional arguments that what is must be.

The scant attention paid to sexual privacy in cultural and social anthropology is all the more puzzling and intriguing because all ethnographers know that wherever in the world they go, they will not be permitted to observe or film actual sexual intercourse among the people with
whom they work. Margaret Mead commented on the human habit of
concealed sex back in 1961 as part of a discussion of the difficulties of
obtaining cross-cultural information on sex acts (1961:1434–35), a situation also noted by Symons (1979:308). For the most part, however,
the taboo is rarely noticed. On the other hand, we can expect to learn
about the enormous variety of cultural values and attitudes associated

with sex and sexuality, values that are verbalized and symbolized in myriad emotionally charged forms. Apart from rare instances of personal dalliance, not for ethnographic purposes, anthropologists cannot check by direct observation any stories informants tell about their current sexual activities. The most significant value of participant observation—the ability to compare statements about behavior, attitudes, and values with observed actions—is not possible for ordinary sexual acts. The comparison is not possible for compatriots, either (see Tuzin 1991:868–71).[5]

In evolutionary studies by biological anthropologists and paleontologists, concealed sex is considered in attempts to define the differences that distinguish later hominids and *Homo sapiens sapiens* from earlier hominids and the nonhuman primates. The traits usually considered are bipedal locomotion, brain size and function, tool use, the sexual division of labor, burial of the dead, art forms, and speculation about the origins of language. Two sex and reproduction issues come into the discussion. The first is the absence of visible or otherwise easily detectable estrus in human females and the continuous, situation-dependent receptivity to sexual encounters apparently following from it. The second is the human habit of concealing coitus. Both are characterized as distinctly human attributes. Explanations of the origin of the first are common in the literature; explanations of concealed sex are less so. Indeed, these two traits are different in kind. Hidden estrus involves a biologic change in the physiology of human females, a physiologic change that has consequences for sexual behavior. A preference for sex without spectators, in contrast, involves changes in habitual behavior without an apparent change in physiology. It is a practice for which cultural rules have been developed. My concern is with possible precultural conditions for the practice.

Those who attempt to reconstruct the origins of hidden sex face a number of impediments. Obviously neither continuous sexual receptivity nor hidden sexual practices are detectable in the archaeological record. Reconstructions of origins are necessarily speculative and based on indirect evidence. The quest is further complicated because the conditions under which a particular pattern evolves (its origins) cannot stand as the explanation of its persistence or of its current practice, nor are the contemporary functions of a given practice a guaranteed clue to its origins. Nevertheless, I shall discuss origin theories because the exploration of possibilities contributes to a broader understanding of sexuality.

Sociobiology has been the paradigm of choice in most attempts to reconstruct the origins of undetectable estrus and concealed sex. The ultimate goal of animal behavior, according to this view, is reproductive success accomplished by the perpetuation of an individual's own genes or those of his or her close blood kin. Animals are thought to act so as to assist consanguineous kin to maturity, and the actions are considered the driving force of evolution. Encouraging close relatives to reach maturity requires, for most animals, some parental investment in provisioning and protecting helpless young. In mammals maternal investment through gestation and lactation is essential. The level of feeding and protection provided by the male sexual partners of the mother—or, indeed, other males—varies greatly. For primates, the evolutionary road to full humanity is paved by the interaction of increasing brain size and differentiation of brain function, intertwining with tool use and the appearance of language in the context of intense social relations within and between groups.

The scenarios for the development of undetectable ovulation and concealed sex in humans start with the postulate that the large-brained young are born essentially helpless and take a long time to mature in body and mind. Therefore, parental investment must necessarily be serious and prolonged; paternal investment in particular is thought to be essential. Biologists and anthropologists also stress that biologically continuous female sexual receptivity means that females may, if they wish, accept males at any time in the ovulatory cycle, allowing sex to be a constant strong source of attraction between males and females. (It also permits sex acts to be divorced from reproduction.) Competition for mates among males and females alike, together with sexual jealousy, are considered part of human character. The scenarios based on these premises also assume that continuously available sex is a prerequisite for concealed sex. Finally, for most writers, the problem to be solved is how parental investment was infused into human social life. Some authors believe this could not have occurred before changes in the brain led to improved technological skills which, in turn, enabled humans to learn to hunt large game. When meat becomes a significant food source, it is said to trigger a more pronounced division of labor between the sexes. In the words of one writer, "As ecological advantages of hunting and increased paternal care in the reproductive success of both males and females gradually became established in these ancestral creatures by genetic selection, and the pair bond establishing monogamy developed, sex had to become privatized" (Stoddart 1990:227).

The developers of most of the scenarios for the origin of concealed sex actually concentrate on trying to explain the loss of visible or detectable estrus in human females as a way of strengthening the possibilities for parental investment in offspring. Many writers feel that hunting is a prerequisite for loss of estrus because it decreases peak periods of sexual competition and increases male cooperation in hunting. It is said also to enable females to provision their offspring better by trading sex for meat. Another suggestion is that the sense of smell of human males has been desensitized to odors associated with the advertisement of estrus, contributing to concealed estrus (Stoddart 1990:228–29). None of these ideas constitutes a convincing scenario for the development of hidden sex (Diamond 1992:79–84).

In my own view, hypotheses that couple concealed ovulation with concealed sex, under the assumption that the absence of detectable estrus would automatically be followed by concealed sex, are unproductive. Humans are not the only animals who have sex when the female is not ovulating. As Sarah Blaffer Hrdy has shown, sex acts not exclusively for procreation do occur among nonhuman primates, and they are public (1983:145–59). Females may attract males more or less continuously even when there is no concealed estrus. As far as I know, the situation does not result in increased paternal care. In the same vein, occasional acts of hidden sex occur among nonhuman primates that have visible estrus signals and thus only periodic opportunities for sex. Even among these animals, the sex act occurs when procreation cannot follow.[6] What may be far more important for the abolition of estrus signals is the prior increase, for unknown reasons, in the female capacity for orgasm and, perhaps concurrently, desire for intercourse. There is evidence that nonhuman primate females also may have orgasms (Hrdy 1983; see also Eibl-Eibesfeldt 1989:246–47). If female orgasm becomes important, both males and females will be attracted to copulation before, during, and after female fertile periods. Desire may become the proximate cause. Sex for meat could have come later, and hunting would be of less evolutionary significance for the physiological change of loss of estrus.[7]

Now let me turn to a different approach to understanding the possible development of concealed sex. This is an approach that looks not primarily to brain function and body changes as bases for improved technical skills but rather to evolutionary developments that lead to new qualities of *mind*: specifically, to the evolution of social intelligence and the concept of the self. The keys are politics, on the one hand, and the qualities of *mind* and personality necessary for political calculations, on the other. Here, the reported cases of concealed sex among nonhuman primates are again instructive. The pattern is for a couple to hide from the view of other animals that might object to the sexual liaison. For example, a rhesus monkey female follows a male that is not from her troop when he walks out of sight, looking around all the while to make sure no one is watching. Her own adult troop members would interfere with the mating if they saw her (Smuts 1987:407). At Arnhem, in an open-air chimpanzee colony, a subordinate male catches the eye of an estrus female and then looks toward some bushes at the edge of the enclosure. Next he unobtrusively goes out of sight, later followed by the female, and they copulate out of sight. When a third chimpanzee sees the clandestine mating, he rushes to the alpha male to lead him to the locus of the act. In another episode a male takes advantage of two rival males who are preparing action against each other by mating while no one in the troop notices (De Waal 1982:48–50; Zeller 1987:439). It has even been suggested that single-male–multifemale troops might have arisen in breeding sites with unusually good visibility. Males, it is suggested (and I would add females), must be able to monitor the behavior of others and respond instantly (Rowell 1991:63). In any case, the examples suggest that decisions about matings are governed proximately, in the short term, through conscious calculations by the animals of the consequences of their behavior for their social relations within the group. These might be the kind of life history events that help explain evolutionary process.

The particular quality of mind required for the behavior I have just described has been called "social intelligence." It is evident in sexual behavior among humans as well. We share an enhanced capacity to think through the intentions of others and to analyze the behaviors of others in relation to ourselves. Males and females alike form coalitions and friendships informed by visual alertness, curiosity about the world, and flexibility of behavior. Andrew Whiten and Richard Byrne have described one aspect of this capacity as "Machiavellian intelligence" (1988:63), a game of social plot and counterplot that depends on a mental modeling of social relations rather than on observational learning (1988:6). In their attempts to conceal sex, chimpanzees and rhesus monkeys look as if they are trying to deceive other animals. Whiten and Byrne believe that what is predominant in data on social intelligence of nonhuman primates is "the extent to which primate deception is concerned with the perception and manipulation of the attention of others" (Whiten and Byrne 1988:213). This manipulation of attention, when it is meant for concealment or distraction, involves hiding an object (often food) or a person from view or avoiding looking at a desirable object when looking would lead the target to notice it (Whiten and Byrne 1988:213).

The origins of concealing sex may therefore rest on the evolution and development of the social intelligence observed in the nonhuman animals' attempts to deceive their conspecifics in their own interests. While the ultimate consequences may be to improve reproductive success, in my opinion the creators of sociobiological scenarios have not thought through what kind of evolutionary changes were prerequisites for decisions about mating. The development of social intelligence may have been just such a prerequisite, and indeed just as important as the development of technical intelligence. A capacity for politics is already evident in nonhuman primates (De Waal 1982; Schubert and Masters 1991). What may have started as deception to increase reproductive success by avoiding social conflict may have set the stage for evolutionary brain change toward increased ability to calculate consequences of one's acts. I suggest that the social environment may have been conducive to an enhanced capacity for politics—that is, for maneuvers in relation to other animals that require an ability to imagine consequences—and this capacity was a necessary evolutionary prerequisite for the increased utility of private sex. Political skills may have alerted protohumans to the value of hidden sex to protect themselves and the social group from the dangers of jealousy caused by competition both among males and among females for mates. When animals live in groups, a degree of social harmony is a prerequisite for an individual animal's reproductive success.

In humans we need to add another dimension. Human social intelligence, more complex than that of nonhuman primates, requires an evolutionary change that encompasses the appearance of a consciousness of self. Such a change is important because a consciousness of self has few if any relevant precursors in the animal world. Chimpanzee behavior is once again instructive. Most animals placed in front of a mirror do not recognize themselves in their reflection, instead reacting as if they were seeing another animal. Chimpanzees are, as far as we know, the only nonhuman primates who discover, after a few tries at attacking or posturing before what they think at first is another animal in the mirror, that it is themselves they see. It has been argued that chimpanzees may possess a cognitive category for processing mirrored information about the self. They appear to have as a consciousness of self; they are self-aware (Gallup 1982:240, 242). Humans are, of course, quintessentially so, as Hallowell pointed out long ago (1954:106).

Among humans sex acts are a significant source of a person's consciousness of self and perception of self. Coitus is prolonged in contrast to the acts of many primates. A private setting for intimacy during intercourse permits constraints to disappear, and self-absorption is enhanced (Knight 1991:151–52). Such self-absorption increases the sense of self; a violation of privacy diminishes the self. Therefore, I propose that if there is an evolutionary adaptive base for invisible sex, it must be understood in terms of selection for the psychological and cognitive characteristics of intelligence and mind that enhance the capacity for mental modeling of social relations, in which the maintenance of self is an important part (Symons 1987, 1992:150). Undetectable estrus may then be considered a corequisite with hidden sex. Indeed, concealment could then, in turn, help cement bonds between sex partners and become a boundary-making mechanism, distinguishing sexual partners from other members of the social group (Diamond 1992:83–84; Frayser 1985:117).

I wish now to consider the consequences of hidden sex, whatever its origin. I think it important to think about what might inevitably follow from the establishment of a near universal pattern of hidden sex activity among humans. I shall discuss only three consequences: the need for children to learn about sex without the help of direct observation, the psychological effect of invisibility, and the mutual vulnerabilities hidden sex creates for sex partners.

For children, one consequence of hidden sex is that they do not, under ordinary circumstances, acquire their knowledge of sex acts by direct observation of other humans. Children in the same space as adults can see motions under covers and hear sounds in the dark, but the mechanics may remain a mystery. In societies where wild or domesticated animals are observed to copulate, children can learn and talk about the analogies with humans. Even then, the rear entry position of animals is not a model for the frontal sex of most humans. When sex takes place in the bush, children sometimes sneak up and spy and may not be punished for their curiosity. Folklore of both frightening and humorous sorts informs youngsters, as do other children's tales. Parents—and, in literate societies, books, schools, sex manuals, and pornography—also instruct. Some of what is learned is inaccurate not only in terms of scientific knowledge but even in terms of a person's own society's practices (Gagnon and Simon 1973:112–18).

In some societies—especially where sex is viewed as defiling, wicked, and to be engaged in only for procreation—it is even possible for some children to grow up ignorant of sex and sexuality, with their knowledge of coitus wholly distorted and remaining a total mystery. Hidden sex may foster such ignorance. Surprisingly, during the Second World War, social workers at a U.S. Army camp told me that they regularly saw married couples who came to them for help because they simply did not know what to do to consummate their marriages. In any case, hidden sex complicates the emotional and psychological life of children who must somehow learn its secrets. In our own times, ignorance or misinformation about the mechanics of sex and their relation to procreation and to sexually transmitted diseases is life threatening to people the world over. Sex education can save lives!

The second consequence of hidden sex I shall discuss is the psychological affect associated with invisibility. The very words used to describe the phenomenon give us a clue: hidden, concealed, secret, private. Private and privacy, I believe, are key words for invisible sex. I shall use the meanings associated with private acts to reveal the affective consequences of hidden sex. I am aware that many societies do not have a culturally articulated notion of privacy, though their members do engage in private acts. As a first approximation for the purposes of this essay, I use the writings of some legal scholars in the United States as a useful way to start to think about the issues. A number of these scholars associate privacy with secrecy and duplicity, among other attributes, but they also consider it an essential requirement for creating a sense of self. Let me give a few examples.

Stanley Benn prefaces his essay in the anthology *Privacy, Freedom, and Respect for Persons* with the ditty on bird watching with which I introduced this article. For him, the epitome of privacy is the hidden act of sex. Benn writes that the general principle of privacy might be grounded in the more general principle of respect for persons: "By a person I understand a subject with a consciousness of himself as agent, who is capable of having projects and assessing his achievements in relation to them" (1971:8). He adds that "once a social norm declares certain acts as private it is embarrassing to be seen doing them" (1971:15). Sissela Bok, in her book on secrecy, argues that the distinguishing feature of secrecy is hiding; she distinguishes it from privacy, which is a condition of being protected from unwanted access by others (1982: 11). When control of access has to be hidden, secrecy and privacy overlap. She says that secrecy, though it is needed for human survival, for autonomy and identity, "enhances every form of abuse" (1982:6). Aspects of the underlying experience of secrecy are the sacred, the silent, the forbidden, and the stealthy (Bok 1982:14). Ferdinand Schoeman argues that privacy is suspect as a value because it makes deception possible and enables individuals to conceal things about which they are ashamed or guilty. Yet a sense of self, he contends, is not possible without privacy (1984:403). Benn makes much the same point, quoting Sartre's comment that a necessary condition for knowing oneself as anything at all is that one should conceive of oneself as an object of scrutiny (1971:7). Ruth Gavison suggests that privacy allows individuals to have control over editing themselves, to create themselves on their own terms (1980:450).

Consider, then, that although every private act of sex may be a significant opportunity for an individual to self-create (as well as to procreate) and to develop an intimate association with another while enhancing sense of self, it has also the potential for strong negative associations. Whatever the culture, secrecy and privacy are thought to allow for deceit, lies, prurient curiosity, and even arousal. Simon and Gagnon have described the separation of everyday identity from erotic identity as a highly disjunctive experience—not to be seen, not to see, not to be seen seeing. In seeking the answer to who one is during sex with another, one's everyday identity is reduced to that of coconspirator (1987:371). The conspiracy, in some societies, is expected to be a bond of love and affection and humor, self-enhancing in the best way. It can assuage desire. Or it may be a cover for abuse. Sexual partners, then, whether they be male and female or homosexual couples, are locked into a suspicious, technically intimate relationship about which they alone have knowledge. They are in each other's power.

This circumstance leads to a third consequence of invisible sex, the vulnerability of each sex partner to the other. Ruth Bleier writes that sexuality can be perceived as a measure of one's attractiveness to other people, as a route to intimacy, as the way to be entrusted with another's vulnerability (1984:166). There is strong agreement that people experience their sexuality as self-defining and that sexuality is linked to identity (Person 1987:400). The author of a textbook on sexuality for nurses comments that sex, when kept private, is fertile ground for shame and gives testimony to its self-revealing character (Hogan 1985:202). Most importantly, sexual intercourse means making known to another some previously unknown aspect of the self (Reiss 1986:33–34). Surprisingly, discussions do not mention the acute poignancy of the revelation of one's masculinity and femininity to a sex partner. Whatever economic, political, social, or ritual practices and symbolic associations cultural systems construct for genders, performance in intercourse is certainly everywhere part of the list. For those not involved in the act, the most patent measure of accomplishment for heterosexual partners is the pregnancy of the woman. It is a visible sign of an invisible act.

Because of its private nature, there can be great variability from prescribed norms in every society in actual sexual practices (Tuzin 1991: 870–74). Impregnation may be achieved by the robust participation of both partners, by a man's coercion of the woman, by a woman's skill in arousing her partner and vice versa, by experimentation with techniques that enhance enjoyment as well as impregnation, by frequent acts of sex or by few. Sometimes the techniques or frequencies do not accord with what are defined as morally correct by the dictates of the culture, and there is a range of differences in the physical characteristics of male and female genitals and other erogenous zones, which become apparent to the partners in a sex act. Only the individuals engaged in the act have these kinds of knowledge of each other and, consequently, power over each other through this knowledge. Their secrets remain private unless one tells on the other. Hidden sex makes them vulnerable to each other.

The vulnerability is even more extreme in situations where pregnancy is neither a desire nor a possible outcome: in premarital sex, in adulterous relations, and, in some societies, in homosexual relations. In these cases not only is the nature and quality of the performance secret but the very existence of an act of sex must be kept hidden by deception and lies. Some prominent contemporary cases of the vulnerability of one partner to another who threatens to tell all easily come to mind—and how much worse when someone does indeed tell all. But then, who knows? There are no witnesses. The bugs, tape recorders, and secret television camera are all testaments to the impediments in seeing or gazing on sex; and certainly the difficulty of obtaining conviction for rape is another. In every society gossip about people's personal lives is fueled by the secrecy of sex. Male boasting about prowess is always possible, and who's to tell except his partner. A woman's frigidity or happy pleasure can remain hidden if she wishes, unless her lover speaks up. So everyone can lie a little.

It is ironic that the hiding of sex, which may have begun as a practice to enable animals to protect themselves from harassment from other animals and to maintain political, social, and economic relations without the disruptions of open sexual competition, may end in creating an arena of private innuendos and possible accusations. It is equally ironic that the actualization of the self, with the potential for intimate love—the very process of establishing identity that is such a strong quality in humans, and one that the private sex act enhances for both partners—has the sting of perfidy in its tail. I submit that the consequences of invisible sex contribute universally to wariness and guardedness between men and women. Men may have power, but even in strongly patriarchal societies, it is possible for their female sex partners to contradict their claims to sexual prowess, and the men can become subjects of gossip. A woman's femininity is in jeopardy if she cannot attract or satisfy a man, whether or not she gets pregnant. These possibilities hold regardless of whether marriages are arranged or property changes hands and regardless of the economic, political, or family influence men and women have in a society—nor do they depend on the symbolic cultural meaning given to sexuality by each culture. The wariness and the ambiguity engendered by private sexual acts serve as an underlying theme of gender relations on which cultural variations are constructed.

In the search for humanity and human nature, I chose some years ago to start thinking about a particular set of persons and relationships, almost universal among humans, and to speculate on the possibility that they might have spawned particular types of psychological relations between sex partners. In so doing, I have assumed that social relations preceded cultural rules and cultural understandings and symbols about acts of sex (Carrithers 1992:34). With such a point of view, an evolutionary perspective has made sense. I hope that the exercise will contribute new bases for an understanding of the enormous range of human individual and cultural variation in rules and beliefs about sex and encourage the search for more similarities.

NOTES

Reproduced by permission of the American Anthropological Association from *American Anthropologist* 96:4, December 1994. Not for further reproduction. This article is a revised version of a distinguished lecture given for the General Anthropology Division of the American Anthropological Association on November 19, 1993. I want to thank Ingrid Byerly, Haven White, and Katherine Barrett-Gaines for their help in collecting material for this article. I am also grateful for the chance to present the essay at the Duke Department of Cultural Anthropology Monday Colloquium and the Duke Women's Studies Faculty Seminar, where I received excellent criticism and advice. I owe thanks too for conversations with Robert I. Levy, Shirley Lindenbaum, Peter and Jane Schneider, Andrew Scott, Judith Shapiro, and Barbara Hernstein Smith. Muriel Dimen provided a long and thoughtful critique for which I am especially grateful. I am indebted also to Merel Harmel for his editorial skills and encouragement. Some anonymous reviewers gave excellent advice. The final product is, of course, solely my responsibility.

1. For the view that sexuality is only a social construct, see Foucault 1980: 152 and Kon 1987:257.

2. Sexually significant or erotic acts are not limited to genital intercourse but can include fellatio, anal intercourse, and the like, which are usually also hidden. There is cultural variation with respect to whether or not caressing, petting, kissing, and other possibly erotic behaviors are considered appropriate when there is an audience. In this article I do not purport to explore all aspects of human sexuality but limit the discussion to coitus.

3. See Brown 1991:39, 150; Davenport 1977:150; Endleman 1988:38; Ford and Beach 1951:68; Foucault 1980:3; and Morgan 1907:473.

4. Nevertheless, a report on a conference on human sexuality quotes one participant who omits the ubiquity of hidden sex from his roster of human universals. It is not clear whether the omission was deliberate or inadvertent (Okami and Pendleton 1994:89).

5. Defecation is another bodily function frequently thought to be inappropriate in public, and it also needs anthropological attention. In the sense that it involves the hiding of certain body parts and may be associated with shame, comparisons with hidden sex could be fruitful. However, defecation with spectators is culturally permitted in enough societies and under enough circumstances that it is usually not listed among human universals.

6. The examination of nonhuman primate sex behavior as an aid to understanding human sex behavior has often been questioned (Okami and Pendleton 1994:88). Historically, we have indeed been known to interpret primate behavior in terms of the scholars' versions of human sexual and gender patterns. The danger of doing so continues. Can we avoid such circularity? Probably not entirely, but nonhuman primates are sufficiently similar to humans so that we can use their actions to develop hypotheses about human behavior. Those hypotheses can then be tested in the usual ways. It is in this spirit that I use nonhuman primate behavior for comparison and inspiration in this article.

7. Other attempts to explain the evolution of human sexuality through female physiological change refer to the relatively prolonged and heavy menstruation of females compared to other animals and the phenomenon of synchronized menstrual period among women living in close quarters (Knight 1991:13–14; Turke 1984:33–36). They assume that once hunting developed, females synchronized menstruation to encourage males to engage in activities other than sex and thus increase hunting time. The thesis depends on the unwarranted assumption that sex is avoided during menstruation. This is not the case in many human societies and need not have been in protohominid or early hominid forms.

REFERENCES

Alland, A. 1972. *The Human Imperative*. New York: Columbia University Press.

Benn, S. I. 1971. Privacy, Freedom, and Respect for Persons. In *Privacy*, ed. J. R. Pennock and J. W. Chapman, pp. 1–26. New York: Atherton.

Bleier, R. 1984. *Science and Gender: A Critique of Biology and Its Theories*. New York: Pergamon.

Bok, S. 1982. *Secrets: On the Ethics of Concealment and Revelation*. New York: Pantheon.

Brown, D. E. 1991. *Human Universals*. New York: McGraw-Hill.

Brundage, J. S. 1987. *Law, Sex, and Christian Society in Medieval Europe*. Chicago: University of Chicago Press.

Byrne, R. W., and A. Whiten, eds. 1988. *Machiavellian Intelligence: Social Expertise and the Evolution of the Intellect in Monkeys, Apes, and Humans*. Oxford: Clarendon Press.

Carrithers, M. 1992. *Why Humans Have Cultures: Explaining Anthropology and Social Diversity*. New York: Oxford University Press.

Davenport, W. H. 1977. Sex in Cross-Cultural Perspective. In *Human Sexuality in Four Perspectives*, ed. F. A. Beach, pp. 115–53. Baltimore: Johns Hopkins University Press.

De Waal, F. 1982. *Chimpanzee Politics: Power and Sex Among Apes*. New York: Harper and Row.

Diamond, J. 1992. *The Third Chimpanzee: The Evolution and Future of the Human Animal*. New York: Harper Collins.

Eibl-Eibesfeldt, I. 1989. *Human Ethology*. New York: Aldine de Gruyter.

Endleman, R. 1988. Love: Transcultural Considerations. In *Love: Psychoanalytic Perspectives*, ed. J. F. Lasky and H. W. Silverman, pp. 31–51. New York: New York University Press.

Fisher, H. E. 1982. *The Sex Contract: The Evolution of Human Behavior*. New York: Quill.

Ford, C., and F. A. Beach. 1951. *Patterns of Sexual Behavior*. New York: Harper and Brothers.

Foucault, M. 1980. *The History of Human Sexuality, Volume One: An Introduction*. New York: Vintage.

Frayser, S. G. 1985. *Varieties of Sexual Experience: An Anthropological Perspective on Human Sexuality*. New Haven, Conn.: HRAF Press.

Gagnon, J. H., and W. Simon. 1973. *Sexual Conduct: The Social Sources of Human Sexuality*. Chicago: Aldine.

Gallup, G. G. 1982. Self-Awareness and the Emergence of Mind in Primates. *American Journal of Primatology* 2:237–48.

Gavison, R. 1980. Privacy and the Limits of Law. *Yale Law Journal* 89: 421–71.

Hallowell, A. I. 1954. The Self and Its Behavioral Environment. *Explorations* 2:106–65.

Hogan, R. 1985. *Human Sexuality: A Nursing Perspective*. Norwalk, Conn.: Appleton-Century-Crofts.

Hrdy, S. B. 1983. *The Woman That Never Evolved*. Cambridge: Harvard University Press.

Knight, C. 1991. *Blood Relations: Menstruation and the Origins of Culture.* New Haven: Yale University Press.

Kon, I. S. 1987. A Sociocultural Approach. In *Theories of Human Sexuality*, ed. J. H. Geer and W. T. O'Donohue, pp. 257–86. New York: Plenum.

Lee, R. B. 1979. *The Kung San: Men, Women, and Work in a Foraging Society.* New York: Cambridge University Press.

Mead, M. 1961. Cultural Determinants of Sexual Behavior. In *Sex and Internal Secretions*, ed. W. C. Young, pp. 1433–79. Baltimore: Williams and Wilkins.

Morgan, L. H. *Ancient Society.* New York: Henry Holt.

Okami, P., and L. Pendleton. 1994. Theorizing Sexuality: Seeds of a Transdisciplinary Paradigm Shift. *Current Anthropology* 35:85–94.

Person, E. S. 1987. A Psychoanalytical Approach. In *Theories of Human Sexuality*, ed. J. H. Geer and W. T. O'Donohue, pp. 385–410. New York: Plenum.

Reiss, I. L. 1986. *Journey into Sexuality: An Exploratory Voyage.* Englewood Cliffs, N.J.: Prentice-Hall.

Rowell, T. E. 1991. On the Significance of the Concept of the Harem When Applied to Animals. In *Primate Politics*, ed. G. Schubert and R. D. Masters, pp. 57–72. Carbondale: Southern Illinois University Press.

Schoeman, F. D. 1984. Privacy and Intimate Information. In *Philosophical Dimensions of Privacy: An Anthology*, ed. F. D. Schoeman, pp. 403–18. Cambridge: Cambridge University Press.

Schubert, G., and R. D. Masters, eds. 1991. *Primate Politics.* Carbondale: Southern Illinois University Press.

Simon, W., and J. H. Gagnon. 1987. A Sexual Scripts Approach. In *Theories of Human Sexuality*, ed. J. H. Geer and W. T. O'Donohue, pp. 363–82. New York: Plenum.

Smith, J. R., and L. G. Smith. 1971 [1970]. Co-Marital Sex and the Sexual Freedom Movement. In *Human Sexual Behavior*, ed. B. Lieberman, pp. 281–88. New York: John Wiley.

Smuts, B. 1987. Gender, Aggression, and Influence. In *Primate Societies*, ed. B. Smuts et al., pp. 400–411. Chicago: University of Chicago Press.

Stoddart, D. M. 1990. *The Scented Ape: The Biology and Culture of Human Odour.* New York: Cambridge University Press.

Symons, D. 1979. *The Evolution of Human Sexuality.* New York: Oxford University Press.

———. 1987. An Evolutionary Approach: Can Darwin's View of Life Shed Light on Human Sexuality? In *Theories of Human Sexuality*, ed. J. H. Geer and W. T. O'Donohue, pp. 91–126. New York: Plenum.

————. 1992. On the Use and Misuse of Darwinism in the Study of Human Behavior. In *The Adapted Mind*, ed. J. H. Barkow, L. Cosmides, and J. Tooby, pp. 137–62. New York: Oxford University Press.

Turke, P. 1984. Effects of Ovulatory Concealment and Synchrony on Proto-hominid Mating Systems and Parental Roles. *Ethology and Sociobiology* 5:33–44.

Tuzin, D. 1991. Sex, Culture and the Anthropologist. *Social Science and Medicine* 33:867–74.

Whiten, A., and R. W. Byrne. 1988. The Manipulation of Attention in Primate Tactical Deception. In *Machiavellian Intelligence*, ed. R. W. Byrne and A. Whiten, pp. 211–23. Oxford: Clarendon Press.

Zeller, A. C. 1987. Communication by Sight and Smell. In *Primate Societies*, ed. B. Smuts et al., pp. 433–39. Chicago: University of Chicago Press.

Contributors

ERNESTINE FRIEDL is the James B. Duke Professor Emeritus in the Department of Cultural Anthropology at Duke University. She received her Ph.D. from Columbia University in 1950. She has done fieldwork among the Chippewa of Wisconsin and in rural Greek villages. Since the late 1960s Friedl has pursued an interest in gender studies. She is past president of the American Anthropological Association.

SUZANNE G. FRAYSER is an independent social science consultant and visiting lecturer at Colorado College. She received her Ph.D. from Cornell University in social anthropology in 1976. Much of her work has focused on cross-cultural studies of human sexuality. In addition to many articles in cross-cultural studies, her books include *Studies in Human Sexuality*, with T. J. Whitby, and *Varieties of Sexual Experience*.

GILBERT HERDT is a professor on the Committee for Human Development at the University of Chicago. He received the Ph.D. in anthropology from Australian National University in 1978. He has authored, coauthored, and edited over thirty articles and chapters and eighteen books. His most recent publications are *Same Sex, Different Cultures* and *Sexual Cultures, Migration, and AIDS*.

WILLIAM JANKOWIAK is an associate professor of anthropology at the University of Nevada, Las Vegas. He received the Ph.D. from the University of California, Santa Barbara in 1986. He has conducted extensive field research in China and North America. Jankowiak is the author of numerous scientific publications, including *Sex, Death, and Hierarchy in a Chinese City* and *Romantic Passion*. He is currently working on a book about life in a contemporary American polygamous community.

ANDREW W. MIRACLE is professor and chair of the Department of Health Sciences at Cleveland State University. He received the M.A. in Latin American studies in 1973 and the Ph.D. in anthropology in 1976 from the University of Florida. He has authored or edited eight volumes and written over fifty articles and chapters. His current research focuses on the cross-cultural relationships among sports, rape, and warfare.

DAVID N. SUGGS is an associate professor of anthropology and director of African and African American studies at Kenyon College. He received the Ph.D. in cultural anthropology from the University of Florida in 1986. Suggs has conducted extensive field research in Botswana, much of it focusing on the construction of gender, life course, and alcohol consumption. He is the coeditor, with Andrew Miracle, of *Culture and Sexuality*.

LINDA D. WOLFE is professor and chair of the Department of Anthropology at East Carolina University. She received the Ph.D. from the University of Oregon in 1976. She has conducted field research on monkeys in Japan and India. Wolfe has published many articles on free-ranging rhesus and Japanese monkeys and coedited *Biological Anthropology: The State of the Science* with Noel Boaz. She is currently investigating social networks in semi-free-ranging ringtail lemurs at the Duke University Primate Center.

CAROL M. WORTHMAN is an associate professor of anthropology and director of the Laboratory of Comparative Human Biology at Emory University. She received her Ph.D. from Harvard University in 1978. She has done extensive biocultural research with adolescents in Africa and the Americas. Much of her work has focused on human reproduction and human development.